WORLD BANK TECHNICAL PAPER

Managing Catastrophic Disaster Risks Using Alternative Risk Financing and Pooled Insurance Structures

John D. Pollner

The World Bank
Washington, D.C.

Technical Papers are published to communicate the results of the Bank's work to the development community with the least possible delay. The typescript of this paper therefore has not been prepared in accordance with the procedures appropriate to formal printed texts, and the World Bank accepts no responsibility for errors. Some sources cited in this paper may be informal documents that are not readily available.

The findings, interpretations, and conclusions expressed in this paper are entirely those of the author(s) and should not be attributed in any manner to the World Bank, to its affiliated organizations, or to members of its Board of Executive Directors or the countries they represent. The World Bank does not guarantee the accuracy of the data included in this publication and accepts no responsibility for any consequence of their use. The boundaries, colors, denominations, and other information shown on any map in this volume do not imply on the part of the World Bank Group any judgment on the legal status of any territory or the endorsement or acceptance of such boundaries.

The material in this publication is copyrighted. The World Bank encourages dissemination of its work and will normally grant permission promptly.

Permission to photocopy items for internal or personal use, for the internal or personal use of specific clients, or for educational classroom use, is granted by the World Bank, provided that the appropriate fee is paid directly to Copyright Clearance Center, Inc., 222 Rosewood Drive, Danvers, MA 01923, U.S.A., telephone 978-750-8400, fax 978-750-4470. Please contact the Copyright Clearance Center before photocopying items.

For permission to reprint individual articles or chapters, please fax your request with complete information to the Republication Department, Copyright Clearance Center, fax 978-750-4470.

All other queries on rights and licenses should be addressed to the World Bank at the address above or faxed to 202-522-2422.

ISBN: 0-8213-4917-1
ISSN: 0253-7494

John D. Pollner is a senior financial sector specialist in the Financial Sector Development Department at the World Bank.

Library of Congress Cataloging-in-Publication Data

Pollner, John D., 1957-
   Managing catastrophic disaster risk using alternative risk financing and pooled insurance
structures / John D. Pollner.
      p.   cm. — (World Bank technical paper ; no. 495)
   Includes bibliographical references
   ISBN 0-8213-4917-1
   1. Insurance, Disaster—Caribbean Area.   2. Risk management—Caribbean Area.
3. Reinsurance—Caribbean Area.   I. Title.   II. Series.

HG9979.4.C27 P65   2001
368.1'22'009729—dc21   2001020259

CONTENTS

Foreword

The active risk management of natural disasters at a countrywide level is becoming a legitimate activity for governments and development agencies around the world. It is true that many governments have the taxing power and wherewithal to re-deploy resources throughout an economy to pay for natural disaster losses, however this capacity relies on the existence of tax bases which are significantly higher in proportion to GDP and more widely diversified than those of most developing countries. In addition in many industrial countries there is a well established private sector insurance mechanism in place to spread risk throughout the community and internationally. In many developing countries the insurance sector is only at a nascent stage of development.

Given a lack of local resources and institutions, many of the most vulnerable countries have relied on external aid and post disaster funding to deal with natural disasters. However these funding sources can no longer be taken for granted, partly because of limited supply against a growing demand, but also because the fiscal position of a number of countries limits the scope for heavy further borrowing, particularly in a post disaster environment. In addition there is clear evidence that funds which can be quickly released have a disproportionately beneficial impact on a traumatized economy and population, and this points to alternative approaches.

In this context a wide range of long established and recently developed pre funding and risk hedging instruments have become available for country level risk management. In particular these provide a promising suite of policy tools, sometimes in combination with development bank instruments, for the amelioration of financial shocks arising from natural disasters. Before these can be applied however a full risk profile of the country needs to be prepared. The assessment underlying this profile involves an exhaustive study of hazard frequencies and intensities, the stock of capital at risk, its structural characteristics, and other measures of vulnerability.

The multilateral community's role includes coordinating governments, local private sectors, and international financial markets, in order to help structure the most cost effective disaster funding mechanisms for vulnerable countries. Another potential role in the funding area could be to provide adequate liquidity support in order to catalyze the development of domestic institutions and instruments and hence promote improved country risk management. This report explores these issues in the context of hurricane prone countries in the Eastern Caribbean, and proposes options and financial arrangements which could accommodate the risk transfer needs of governments and the private sector.

Rodney Lester
Lead Specialist and Head, Insurance and
Contractual Savings Common Anchor Team
Financial Sector Development Department
The World Bank

Acknowledgments

This report was produced by a team headed by John D. Pollner, Task Manager and Senior Financial Sector Specialist of the Finance Unit in the Latin America and the Caribbean Regional Office of the World Bank. The core technical team members were Vijay Kalavakonda (Financial Analyst, Insurance Unit, FSD), Arthur Evans (Insurance Consultant), Rodney Lester (Lead Specialist and Lead Advisor, Insurance Unit, FSD), Don Paterson (CEO, Benfield Greig ReMetrics), and Sean Mooney (Senior VP, Guy Carpenter). Contributing staff included Chris Barham (Sr. Operations, LCSER); P.S. Srinivas (Financial Economist, LCSFF), Philippe Auffret (Economist, LCSPR), Constantine Symeonides-Tsatsos (Country Officer); Jean Michel Attlan (Sr. Insurance Officer, Disaster Management Facility/IFC); and Modibo Camara (Financial Economist, LCSFF).

The principal author of this report was John Pollner (World Bank). Contributing co-authors were Sean Mooney (Guy Carpenter) and Arthur Evans (Insurance Consultant). Essential technical information on financial structures and innovations in the catastrophe insurance market were kindly provided by Emilio Fernando (Managing Director, Chase Securities Inc.); and Michael Millette (Vice President, Goldman Sachs).

The Country Director for this work was Orsalia Kalantzopoulos and the Sector Director was Danny Leipziger, World Bank. The Sector Manager for the Finance Cluster was Fernando Montes-Negret and the Regional Financial Sector Adviser was Augusto de la Torre. The Regional Chief Economist was Guillermo Perry.

The report could not have been produced without the valuable technical research and substantive financial and insurance industry analytical contributions received from Goldman Sachs and Co., Guy Carpenter/Marsh McLennan; Benfield Greig Ltd., Chase Manhattan Bank, and the Insurance Information Institute of New York.

Technical contributions and information supporting the report's research were also provided by Norris Stubbs, Professor and Insurance Engineer, Texas A and M University; Michael Murray, Assistant Vice President at the U.S. Insurance Services Office; Jan Vermeiren, Principal Specialist at the Organization of American States; Morton Lane, President, Sedgwick Lane Financial; Neil Doherty, Professor of Risk Management Sciences at the Wharton School of the University of Pennsylvania; Tony Gibbs, CEP Engineering, Barbados, and Mina Hamedani, Risk Securitization Consultant.

We wish to thank the Governments, Ministries of Finance, Insurance Supervisors and Insurance Industry representatives of Antigua and Barbuda, Barbados, Dominica, Grenada, St. Kitts and Nevis, St. Lucia, St. Vincent and the Grenadines, and Trinidad and Tobago, for their valuable assistance and feedback regarding the detailed characteristics and experience of the Caribbean insurance markets.

Editorial Note: This report utilizes the abbreviation 'ESC' to mean 'East Caribbean'. The term is used differently from EC or Eastern Caribbean which is commonly used to refer to the OECS countries or countries in the ECCB Area. As this report covers the OECS countries as well as Barbados and Trinidad and Tobago, when referring to all these countries as a sub-regional group, the term ESC has been adopted.

ABBREVIATIONS AND ACRONYMS

BLP	Barbados Light and Power Co. Ltd.
CARICOM	Caribbean Community
CARILEC	Caribbean Electric Utilities Service Corporation
CAT	Catastrophe
CCR	Caisse Centrale de Reassurance
CEA	California Earthquake Authority
CHA	Caribbean Hotel Association
CUBIC	Caribbean Uniform Building Code
EC	Eastern Caribbean
ECCB	Eastern Caribbean Central Bank
ESC	East Caribbean (OECS, Barbados, Trinidad and Tobago)
EPL	Estimated Expected Loss
FM	Factory Mutual
FAIR	Fair Access to Insurance Requirements
FJUA	Florida Joint Underwriting Association
GAAP	Generally Accepted Accounting Principles
GDP	Gross Domestic Product
IAC	Insurance Association of the Caribbean
IBRD	International Bank for Reconstruction and Development
IFC	International Finance Corporation
III	Insurance Information Institute
IRI	Industrial Risks Insurers
HHRF	Hawaii Hurricane Relief Fund
JER	Japanese Earthquake Reinsurance Co.
JUA	Joint Underwriting Association
LIBOR	London Interbank Offer Rate
MAP	Market Assistance Plan
MPH	Miles Per Hour
OAS	Organization of American States
OECS	Organization of Eastern Caribbean States
PCS	Property Claim Service
P+I	Principal and Interest
PML	Probable Maximum Loss
ROL	Rate on Line (reinsurance price)
SPV	Special Purpose Vehicle
T&D	Transmission and Distribution
VR	Vulnerability Reduction
WTO	World Trade Organization
XL	Excess of Loss (reinsurance contract/cover)

EXECUTIVE SUMMARY

Caribbean nations on the whole, are exposed to high levels of risk from natural disasters, primarily hurricane and windstorm risks, but also significant concentrations of earthquake, volcano, and flood risks.

As part of a historical strategy to address the financial and economic impact of such risks, many Caribbean islands have successfully leveraged international insurance capital and have been able to transfer much of the risk, particularly for commercial but also residential properties, on to the international insurance and reinsurance markets. The same has not been the case, however, for public sector assets and infrastructure, many of which remain heavily exposed and implying large potential fiscal liabilities if natural catastrophes were to disable such assets.

Improving Risk Sharing For Catastrophic Losses: A Structured Finance Approach With Developmental Benefits

For developing economies subject to natural disasters, and to meet the long term sustainable growth objectives of small economies, this report addresses the available mechanisms for utilizing and improving the insurance market to handle disaster risks.

The report critically examines the current financial and insurance institutions in both emerging and developed economies, and concludes that with key institutional changes, catastrophe losses can be better absorbed by markets, with resulting financial benefits to local industries, domestic insurance companies, households, international reinsurers, and governments, through the use of more optimally structured risk sharing arrangements. This approach is consistent with global trends in reducing the role of the state which is traditionally a significant sector in small countries, and hence more vulnerable.

The conclusion, based on the evidence, is that market arrangements (both domestic and international) can better channel and fund these risks, with governments and multilateral institutions supporting the development of self-sustaining structures. Market mechanisms for disaster funding do not always develop on their own precisely because they have, historically, interfaced among local institutions and the gargantuan international markets, hence the role of multilateral development institutions as international facilitators for improving the functioning of risk transfer mechanisms.

The analysis contained in this report using conservative financial assumptions, shows that the structured finance approach is quite feasible with some initial funding leverage to build up the necessary reserve base for ensuring self-sustainability.

Recent Experience in the Catastrophe Insurance Markets

Despite the good use of the international catastrophe reinsurance market as reflected in the well developed albeit thinly capitalized domestic insurance industries in the Caribbean (prompting needed regulatory reforms to achieve higher capital and solvency standards), international market volatility in the last decade has also been a cause of concern regarding the sustainable availability of insurance capital to cover future disaster events in exposed countries.

Global catastrophes such as past hurricanes or earthquakes around the world generated significant reinsurance shortages in the early to mid-1990s resulting in dramatic rate increases in the Caribbean. During the mid 1990s, Caribbean countries experienced insurance rate increases between 200%-300% on account of shortages of insurance cover, due to indemnity payments made for large hurricane and earthquake losses worldwide. From a developmental perspective, this experience of market shocks discouraged prudent 'risk hedging' policies in the form of promoting wider-spread insurance practices both in the public and private sectors of the Caribbean. To illustrate, the average variation on typical catastrophe insurance rates in the Caribbean and internationally, within the past decade, fluctuated between 30% and 50%.

While the latter 1990s experienced welcome decreases in rates after new global insurance companies entered the market and investment bankers began offering securitized insurance instruments for sale in the capital market, the end of volatility, particularly for small countries with a high dependence on foreign coverage, is not necessarily a given. Some worrying signs are the fact that 1998 and 1999 were the years with the highest levels of catastrophic losses from windstorms and earthquakes combined since 1992, the year hurricane Andrew struck Florida and the Caribbean, and 1994, the year of the Northridge earthquake.

Perhaps due to the overly high dependence on the international insurance industry, the local industry of the Caribbean has not accumulated capital of its own to better 'buffer' international rate movements and achieve a more optimal mix of risk-bearing capital, leveraging both domestic and international funds. The domestic insurance industries are generally highly fragmented which accentuates the relatively low levels of available risk capital in a significant portion of the industry. New regulations being developed will raise the bar in terms of minimum capital and underwriting solvency requirements, but additional efforts are needed to ensure that entry into the industry brings additional capacity to better absorb risks.

Another area for development is the adoption of mitigation based pricing incentives since the lack of sufficient risk differentiation for pricing purposes tends to penalize those who have already undertaken productive vulnerability reduction measures. Welcome signs in the regulatory sphere include the tax deductibility of catastrophe insurance reserves in some countries, which help meet the objective of increasing risk bearing capacity.

International Experience with Alternative Risk Transfer Mechanisms

International experiences using alternative catastrophe risk management arrangements have shown that in both public sector sponsored schemes (e.g.: hurricane risk in Hawaii and Florida) or private sector initiatives (investment bank sales of catastrophe insurance linked securities to the global capital markets), innovations have allowed better tailoring of risk bearing capacities and financial terms to those most needing protection, i.e., the insureds as well as the smaller primary insurance companies who are on the front line in identifying and channeling risks to the market. The global capital markets, comprising nearly 50 times the capital of the world insurance markets[1], are well suited to absorb some of the risks and financial payouts generated by catastrophic events.

Various financial market mechanisms have evolved for this purpose, of which 'catastrophe bonds' are a prime example of securitizing insurance risks. Such bonds, which are issued publicly to investors, generally pay interest much above the market rates in order to compensate for the risk of interest or principal defaults by the borrower, in the event of a major catastrophe. However, since the borrower's intermediary can invest the funds in risk free securities (to be used only for a "catastrophe event"), the net cost to the borrower is reduced substantially and approaches that of traditional reinsurance.

In addition, recent innovations such as basing 'disaster payouts' on objective hazard intensity measurements (e.g.: wind speed, earthquake intensity) provide more confidence to investors that underlying damage assessments cannot be manipulated by the borrower/insured, and permit accessibility and transparency in the risk assessment process. Given that such bonds are linked to events unrelated to the traditional financial markets, they also serve as a portfolio diversification hedge for investors. The actuarial probability of default of such bonds is generally lower than similarly rated investment securities already actively traded in the capital markets.

Governments, particularly in the developed economies in Europe and the U.S., have already witnessed the 'exit' of insurers from private markets prone to natural catastrophes and have therefore established public/private collaborative schemes to insure catastrophic cover through risk pooling (and removal of catastrophe risks from company balance sheets), coupled with group reinsurance arrangements and last resort credit back-up. Capital markets have been willing to provide credit support for insurance purposes since projections of future premiums and other charges can suffice to secure such debt and its repayment, if utilized. Thus, capital markets have been able to increase insurance capacity, particularly at the upper loss layers which could strain the balance sheets of insurers and reinsurers alike. For smaller vulnerable economies, such support might be catalyzed by multilateral institutions not only to assure coverage capacity, but also to help stabilize the premiums paid through long term funding arrangements.

To a large extent, however, developing countries facing high risks of natural catastrophe exposure have not had the market access or the industry collaboration required to tap into the latest financial structures and instruments which could optimize their risk coverage and premium terms, taking into account the priority to reduce insurance market volatility and permit sustainable and affordable financial protection. Multilateral institutions can help support the development of broader risk pooling schemes with supporting credit enhancements, to provide actuarially cost effective arrangements to manage catastrophic risks, while promoting efficient markets.

---

[1] Goldman Sachs; U.S. Insurance Services Office, FIBV International Federation of Stock Exchanges, Guy Carpenter / Marsh McLennan.

Addressing the Catastrophe Insurance Problem: Policy and Institutional Responses for Sustainable Risk Management Practices in Disaster Prone Countries

This report demonstrates that in natural disaster prone small economies, difficulties in properly funding potential catastrophic risks, become magnified when compared to the insurance risk challenges already existent in the international markets. Emerging economies suffer not only from the devastating effects of disasters, but also from market imperfections and constraints which generate disincentives to better risk management. In the Caribbean region, the problem of catastrophe risk insurance and constraints to expanding risk management strategies are linked to both the limited domestic risk bearing capacity and the dynamics of international market forces.

The domestic capacity constraints are manifested in: (a) high exposures to perils such a hurricanes, (b) limited fiscal capacities to fund major disaster reconstruction for low income communities and public properties, (c) insufficient vulnerability reduction measures taken for properties and physical assets, (d) limited reserves of domestic insurance capital, and (e) resulting under-insurance in the economy. Closely linked, the characteristics of the international insurance markets have also impacted the development of local risk management practices through: (a) past premium rate volatility which has limited insurance coverage to only middle/higher income sectors, (b) lengthy past delays in rate adjustments and capacity replenishments following global disaster events, (c) high levels of reinsurance provided to local insurers with accompanying commissions remitted which tend to increase incentives for maintaining high premiums, and (d) proportionately higher insurance costs for catastrophic-level risks given insurers' needs to retain high and costly levels of capital to fund such eventualities.

Solutions to the catastrophe risk problem, due to its potentially devastating effects, cannot be accomplished without leveraging sufficient capital and assuring stable long term capacity, two important financial pre-conditions. At the individual country level, governments can instill risk management practices by better controlling 'exposure' through regulatory actions aimed at vulnerability reduction programs particularly for the low income sectors, and by assuring that the local insurance sector has sufficient capital (net of reinsurance cover) to withstand large losses. Simultaneously, enforcement of insurance coverage, both in the private and public sectors is needed, along with market incentives to monitor property risks and adjust premiums by rewarding owners and property holders who reduce physical risk exposures.

While such actions can provide the framework for establishing the requisite institutional support, the magnitude of catastrophe risks requires more radical solutions to ensure that governments can minimize contingent fiscal liabilities and the private sector and local communities can recover quickly from natural disasters. To address the catastrophe-risk insurance constraints listed above, stable insurance funding mechanisms are required with the ability to accumulate reserves which can be more optimally leveraged via risk transfer to the international markets. In the context of small economies with limited risk absorption capacity, the pooling of risk exposures enables broader coverage protection using more efficient deployment of pooled capital for risk transfer, permitting a faster accumulation of catastrophe reserves to help buffer the disruptive supply effects of worldwide disasters on domestic markets.

The resulting efficiencies, including sub-regional diversification and exploiting the latest risk transfer technologies, can be implemented with special credit enhancement instruments to provide backstop liquidity. Such arrangements can be brokered by multilateral development institutions which can assist in arranging the requisite inter-country and market collaboration, while setting the basis for ex ante regulatory requirements to ensure financial solvency and risk reduction. The combination of public, private, international and multilateral resources can jointly implement broader cost effective risk management tools which will begin to minimize, in a more timely manner, the economic and financial disruptions of future disaster events.

The Structure of the Caribbean Insurance Markets

The specific characteristics of existing insurance markets need to be taken into account before considering the structure of pooled or alternative risk financing approaches. In the Caribbean region, the traditional insurance structure involves the proportional treaty contracted with reinsurers, whereby, some 70% of written risks are 'ceded' to reinsurers who take on that proportion of risks as well as the corresponding premium income. For local insurers, however, the transfer of premium income collected is rewarded with commissions paid back by the reinsurers for bringing in and administering the client business. Local insurers also traditionally reinsure another 20% of their retained risk under 'catastrophe excess of loss' (XL) treaties[2]. These are differentiated from proportional or quota share treaties in that they pay no commissions and the premium rate is based on a quantification of a specified limit on payable losses. XL reinsurance, thus requires a more meticulous assessment of risks, exposure and actuarial probabilities. Netting the XL reinsurance cover, Caribbean companies tend to retain a net risk equaling about 20-24% of the total originally insured amounts.

Examining the above arrangements, the analysis shows that increased welfare in terms of reducing individual country risk, can be obtained through pooling such financial risks across different risk zones in the Caribbean. As with portfolio diversification, a larger risk pool not only lowers the minimum net risk capital requirement (and thus increases the surplus capital available), but also allows for more efficient reinsurance arrangements which can be contracted on a larger value base. The analysis of insured loss potentials is a multi-disciplinary effort which takes into account physical weather/geological phenomena, engineering structural analysis, and financial loss estimation. Generally, the estimated expected loss (EPL) is a function of all three, i.e., (a) the probability distribution of hazard events of varying intensities, (b) the structural vulnerability parameters of buildings or physical assets subject to such hazards, and (c) the value of such assets and their associated expected losses in currency terms, when subjected to hazard events and associated structural damages.

However, in the catastrophe insurance industry, given the limited actuarial base (since catastrophe events are defined as extremely infrequent yet severe), the pricing of risk includes an uncertainty factor or 'risk load' which reflects prudent financial management. This means, however, that reinsurance pricing for the upper (least probable) loss levels does not decline in proportion with the scale of loss probability. Thus, the use of capital market instruments such as contingent credit lines can provide certain efficiencies in pricing, since their contractual terms are more binary, that is, during 'no event' periods the price is a minimum commitment charge but after an event, the full principal and interest is repayable. Such pricing efficiencies can be tested both through theoretical financial models such as perpetual annuity present value comparisons, or through time simulations spanning the likely probability periods for major catastrophes.

---

[2] An excess of loss (XL) reinsurance contract claim is invoked when damages exceed a specified amount (the 'attachment point' of the contract). Any losses below the attachment point are 'retained' and paid by the primary insurer. The XL contract, however, only covers losses up to a pre-specified limit (the 'exhaustion point'). Any losses above and beyond that point have to be covered either by the primary insurer or via a different reinsurance contract. In this regard, XL contracts frequently appear as specified 'layers' of coverage within a range of possible loss amounts. In contrast, proportional (quota share) treaties share losses between primary insurer and reinsurer in specified percentages (e.g.: 30% and 70% respectively).

Catastrophe Risk Pooling and Risk Financing Instruments

The World Bank has in the past been involved in the use of contractual, credit and political risk guarantees as part of its available financial instruments to support development. The area of catastrophe insurance is relatively new in this context and therefore, an applicable instrumentation to be considered for specified applications, is examined in this report to support ongoing needs in this recurrent area. The analysis presented demonstrates the feasibility and potential and effectiveness of utilizing Bank instruments to support initiatives which may facilitate corrections in existing market imperfections so as to allow the eventual development of new markets in risk management to serve the needs of emerging economies. Commercial products for the same purpose are also examined -- while these are feasible in the medium term, at the outset some additional prudential longer term protection would be required to avoid potential insolvency of pooled schemes if catastrophes occurred in early years.

The report takes a step-by-step approach to show how both 'risk pooling' structures as well as alternative catastrophe coverage mechanisms in the form of long maturity risk financing facilities and capital market instruments, can achieve more optimal risk protection and financing terms to allow expansion of insured coverage of public sector assets and private properties. Besides testing the straightforward financial engineering aspects of pools supported by credit type instruments, the analysis also examines the effect on domestic and international insurance markets, to ensure that any proposed scheme does not unduly interfere or replace existing market arrangements. By examining the insurable assets (private and public) in eight countries in the easternmost part of the Caribbean, and quantifying the portion of the premium and risk used to fund catastrophe losses, the report shows that, through pooling and use of credit type instruments for catastrophe coverage, governments and uninsured property owners or enterprises (with insurable assets) can expect improved terms of coverage. This can provide greater incentives across countries to promote and implement insurance as a prudent risk management practice in highly exposed areas.

The transfer of a share of catastrophic risks to a pool need not however, imply loss of income to domestic/local insurers. In fact, such a transfer would reduce domestic insurers' largest risks on their retained portfolios which could then be expanded to increase coverage for more traditional non-catastrophic risks. The reduction in the retention of catastrophe risks also would mean that domestic insurers may need less reinsurance protection which would allow them to retain additional gross premium income. While this would appear to reduce the market share of the reinsurers, a pooled scheme would actually have the opposite effect once the coverage capacity was increased to include public sector and other uninsured assets. Since even a regional pooled structure could not fully fund a major catastrophic event, the pool itself would need to reinsure much of its portfolio before it could rely on a backstop credit line at the topmost loss layer. When analyzing the income implications for reinsurers, such a pool with expanded coverage capacity for the assets mentioned, would allow reinsurers to provide additional coverage under more cost effective arrangements for them and for the pool itself, which can be shown to produce net surplus income under the proposed financial structures.

For countries concerned about 'subsidizing' their neighbors under a pooled scheme, this would be prevented by differentiating the price of premiums paid into the pool based on the country and structural risks insured. Concerns of high risk countries using up the pool's initially retained capital before the reinsurance layer can be accessed ('attached'), can be alleviated through financial design options. One such option would permit access to the reinsurance layer in proportion to such countries' risk in the capital (retained) layer. In this manner, any one large disaster would not use up the capital base of the collective pool, although such advantages might be somewhat offset by the higher cost implied by "custom designing" the reinsurance policy for each country.

The use of catastrophe bonds as a top reinsurance layer for a pool, is also examined and considered financially feasible, albeit, slightly more expensive yet still affordable compared to backstop credit at favorable terms. The latter permits an accumulation of substantial savings on premium, thus allowing full funding of the eventual debt service to be paid in the event of a natural catastrophe.

Laying the Foundation with Regulatory and Structural (Physical) Measures

It should be emphasized that, while financial mechanisms may achieve much to optimize the management of large periodic risks affecting the region, regulatory as well as structural measures to lower physical vulnerability need to be also given high priority since such measures can sharply reduce risk exposure in permanent ways. Using the existing engineering expertise and knowledge of Caribbean structural building standards, the analysis goes on to show that with relatively modest investments in vulnerability reduction measures either at the construction stage or retrofitting (the former being more cost effective), the reduction in risk exposure could potentially be as large as 50%.

The risk management options examined can lead to real benefits to all participants (clients and sellers) in the insurance markets. However, some minimum pre-conditions such as (i) a sound and strong insurance regulatory framework, (ii) enforcement of prudent risk management practices, (iii) objective and verifiable criteria for measuring and recording losses, and (iv) implementation and enforcement of protective structural measures and construction codes; are essential for assuring the integrity of any participatory insurance scheme.

The pooling of catastrophe risks also encourages the process of standardization of risk rating and risk assessments which in turn supports the regulatory role of the insurance supervisor. This also helps to counteract the observable fragmentation and varied risk underwriting practices in the domestic insurance sectors, and permits an orderly build up of the necessary catastrophe reserves backed up by more stable multi-year reinsurance and catastrophe financing mechanisms.

Setting a New Paradigm for Disaster Funding from the Development Community

Looking forward, the issue of catastrophe risk management goes beyond the critical needs of particular countries and the functioning of insurance markets, and impacts directly on the existing paradigm of international development assistance. To-date, development institutions both multilateral and bilateral, have focused on ex-post disaster assistance and relief and in essence served as reinsurers of last resort for countries impacted by natural disasters that do not currently employ policies for comprehensive risk management. The mere existence and availability of such external assistance, can generate the same moral hazards that prudent insurance practices attempt to prevent, that is, abdicating the critical practices of ensuring physical protection of assets or not insuring those assets with de facto exposures to natural events.

Nevertheless, the development community has made some progress in the last decade in moving from ex-post disaster reconstruction assistance to a new stage of ex-ante funding for investment in mitigation, as an explicit policy tool for sustainable development. However, to complete the requirements of a national risk management approach, we are now entering a third phase involving the application of risk transfer mechanisms which address the large residual risk of latent exposures to large catastrophic events which require funding means beyond what can be controlled solely through mitigation and physical measures. These residual stochastic risks can better be addressed via the insurance and risk transfer mechanisms which provide the basis for financial protection and instilling strong incentives for vulnerability reduction, both of which can substantially reduce the magnitude of potential economic stresses following disasters.

Structure of the Report

In tackling the challenge of risk management in disaster prone countries, this report examines the existing constraints and opportunities to implement a catastrophe insurance system which can resolve the key obstacles currently impeding broader implementation of a risk funding approach. The four main pillars in such a strategy involve: (i) strengthening the insurance sector regulatory requirements and supervision, (ii) establishment of broad based pooled catastrophe funding structures with efficient risk transfer tools, (iii) promoting public insurance policies linked to programs for loss reduction in the uninsured sectors, and (iv) strengthening the risk assessment and enforcement of structural measures such as zoning and building code compliance.

For this purpose, Chapter I first examines the characteristics of the global insurance and reinsurance market and its links with Caribbean insurers and policyholders, in order to illustrate the local repercussions of world catastrophe events and their impacts on local industry performance. Following that, Chapter II provides an examination of the domestic Caribbean insurance market structure and institutions, and their commercial practices in providing protection to different sectors; showing that the current industry structure may in some cases reduce incentives for improving risk underwriting practices and promoting loss reduction.

Chapter III then discusses how structural mitigation and vulnerability reduction measures can prove to be cost effective investments that can dramatically reduce exposure risks on properties. Such measures which can substantially reduce damages through ex-ante action, can have the effect of lowering property risk premiums through reductions in expected losses. Also examined, is an approach for implementing a public insurance scheme for low income communities in order to promote risk reduction and explicit insurance coverage. Chapter IV then analyzes the modalities of risk transfer for potential financial losses. This includes the specific structure of reinsurance contracts in the Caribbean and the current sharing between domestic risk retention and international risk transfer. The latter demonstrates how the structure of insurance contracts are highly dependent on international capital and its pricing, but allow limited risk underwriting and pricing decision-making at the domestic level.

Chapter V goes on to demonstrate what innovations are being developed for catastrophe risk management, ranging from private securitization of insurance risks to public/private partnerships to increase insurance capacity in constrained markets. This section also demonstrates that the availability of alternative risk financing instruments can be exploited to supplement traditional reinsurance and achieve cost effective means of obtaining coverage and capacity for different levels of catastrophic loss. Chapter VI then examines the options and choices of risk management tools for the ESC and demonstrates that the structuring of inter-country insurance pooling arrangements yields lower aggregate expected losses and improves the leverage provided by risk capital based on the actuarially based exposures to loss, of the individual countries. Such pooled arrangements can provide more coverage capacity and utilize reinsurance and risk financing resources more effectively, due to the resultant economies of scale as well as the improved capacity to accumulate and retain capital reserves.

Chapter VII concludes by demonstrating the financial feasibility and sustainability of operating and managing catastrophe risks under a sub-regional pool. Using historically-based and simulated projections of losses from natural disasters, a catastrophe pool's risk transfer needs can be optimized both with reinsurance as well as alternative risk transfer mechanisms. These can help resolve the issues of adequate coverage and stable funding sources while providing financial incentives and increased underwriting capacity to both domestic insurers and international reinsurers. By-products of this process include the consolidation and monitoring of regulatory solvency for catastrophic risk reserves, and policy leverage to implement loss reduction incentives. The complement of these risk sharing arrangements and risk transfer instruments are tested from a financial feasibility viewpoint to ensure actuarial solvency of a pool. The resulting structure is also shown to allow for increased market participation at both the national and international levels.

I. THE CATASTROPHE INSURANCE AND REINSURANCE MARKETS

This chapter addresses the financial vulnerability of the international reinsurance markets to major global catastrophic events, and the subsequent supply-linked price impacts on the primary insurance industry in the Caribbean. The implication of this analysis is that governments and local insurance industries require financial strategies to better handle potential future fluctuations in these markets in order to maintain sustainable insurance coverage against catastrophic events. For this purpose, protection mechanisms beyond the individual enterprise or specific insurance contract level (topics addressed in the subsequent chapters) can prove to be more beneficial for cushioning global market effects and better leveraging the limited domestic funding base against catastrophic risks. The analysis shows that the increasing risk exposures at the global level as well as the recurrent risks in the Caribbean, will likely perpetuate the volatile insurance cycle. The world capital and credit markets may serve as alternative sources of insurance capital and given their magnitude compared to world insurance markets, such alternatives (discussed further in chapters V and VI) should be considered as available policy tools for countries to improve their effectiveness and efficiency in disaster risk management.

I. THE CATASTROPHE INSURANCE AND REINSURANCE MARKETS

Catastrophe risk poses a unique challenge to the insurance industry, both globally and in the Caribbean. Traditional principles of insurance risk management are based on statistically measurable and predictable distributions of events which allow insurers to finance losses of random occurrences of relatively modest magnitudes through contributions of policy holders. The widely accepted practice of insurance in the world's largest market economies, ironically, reflects a collective method of socializing losses in a way where burden sharing is accepted given the random element of risk at the individual level. However, catastrophic events are much less frequent but very large in terms of loss potential (see figure 1.1). Thus, diversification of such losses is difficult even at a global level where such events have the potential of absorbing huge quantities of capital. This calls for examining the best means of funding risks in catastrophe prone areas and vulnerable states such as the Caribbean islands or other economies prone to natural disasters. The Caribbean is particularly subject to frequent hurricane risks but is also exposed to earthquake and volcanic risks.

Figure 1.1: Statistical Distributions of Loss Probabilities for Normally Distributed Risks Versus Catastrophic Risks

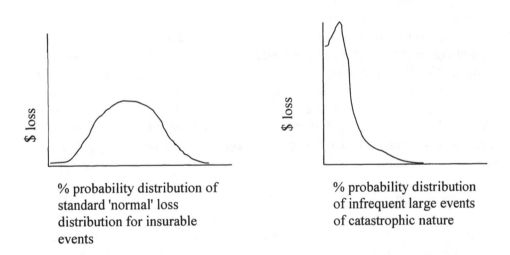

% probability distribution of standard 'normal' loss distribution for insurable events

% probability distribution of infrequent large events of catastrophic nature

The Insurance Services Office of the U.S. highlights the issue of catastrophic risk management, which applies equally to the high risk exposures in U.S. and in the Caribbean: *"The infrequency and high severity of catastrophes contribute to insufficient capital in the property/casualty industry to absorb losses from megacatastrophes. The traditional methods of dealing with large losses from catastrophes, such as reinsurance and guaranty funds, are also inadequate. Individual insurer actions to limit their exposure to catastrophe losses have led to availability problems for insureds in high risk areas. Solutions to the shortage of surplus to manage catastrophe risk, and to availability problems, will require access to capital from outside the industry".* [3]

---

[3] Goldman Sachs, U.S.Insurance Services Office, "Managing Catastrophe Risk", ISO Insurance Issues Series, May 1996.

The same report also states, "The volatility of catastrophe prone lines limits the amount of exposure an insurer can safely write. In the wake of recent catastrophes, insurers are reexamining the extent of their exposure in catastrophe prone areas. Several insurers have attempted to limit the risk to their surplus (capital), leading to local availability problems for the insureds".

The problem of dealing with catastrophic risks is also expressed by Goldman Sachs in its Fixed Income Research series on insurance linked securities: "*Most insurance coverage involves individual events that have a significant economic impact on a single insured entity but are small relative to the reserves of the insurance company providing coverage. The insurance company is able to pool such independent risks and charge premiums based on its administrative costs and its actuarial assessment of the events. In contrast, natural catastrophes such as hurricanes and earthquakes involve a large number of insured entities and have the potential for very large aggregate claims. In contrast to the typical 'high frequency, low severity' risks that insurance companies are easily able to manage, such 'low frequency, high severity' risks present particular difficulties*".

Currently, the insurance industry's capital and surplus in the world stands at close to US$ 1 trillion equivalent. However, major global reinsurers recognize that disaster insurance is severely lacking in many regions of the world, given the actuarial estimates of future events and potential damages. In contrast to the insurance industry, the global capital market capacity stands at approximately US$ 42 trillion or close to 50 times the capital available from the insurance industry, estimated at US$ 850 billion.[4] Therefore, given the increasing concentrations of property values insured as well as scientific projections showing recurring cycles of increased hazard frequencies of hurricanes, it only seems logical that insurance coverage for mega catastrophes will eventually seek capital market financing to complement the limited insurance capital if major events indeed materialize in the next two decades. The instrumentalities for this are elaborated further in chapter IV. Compounding the problem is that dollar-value concentrations of property in catastrophe prone urban areas continue to increase requiring higher and higher amounts of coverage.

At the present time, reinsurance[5] is readily available for most islands in the East Caribbean (ESC) and prices dropped from end-1994 through 1999. However, this situation could change rapidly if a major catastrophe hits the region, or if there is a tightening in world catastrophe reinsurance markets as has begun in early 2000. There are predictions that rates could harden following the relatively active 1999 hurricane season and windstorms at the global level. Not surprisingly, given this volatility in the marketplace, pricing is also highly volatile. After Hurricane Andrew in 1992 which impacted the Florida and Caribbean markets, there was a severe tightening in world catastrophe reinsurance markets, and prices for primary insurance more than doubled in

---

[4]Source: Goldman Sachs, U.S. Insurance Services Office; FIBV International Federation of Stock Exchanges; Guy Carpenter / Marsh McLennan.

[5]The term "reinsurance" refers to the insuring of an insurance company's underwritten portfolio by another larger insurer (the reinsurer). That is, after a primary (or local) insurance company insures its policy holders, it then 'buys' insurance for part of its portfolio from a larger (usually global) company. This is referred to as "reinsurance", i.e., the transferring of part of the original insurer's portfolio to a 'reinsurer' at a price (the reinsurance premium), with the result that the reinsurer takes the risk for that part of the portfolio transferred.

some areas. Since that time, the market has eased and rates continued to fall during 1999. The following rates for a small ESC island, however, are typical of pricing during the 1990s.

Table 1.1: Average Rate for Property Insurance
(Price as basis points of total value insured)

Year	Rate	% change
1990	40	
1994	130	225%
1998	70	(46%)

Source: Insurance Information Institute

However, while the price adjustment increases were swift, due to the capacity constraints the subsequent reduction and stabilization of prices took years, with such adjustments occurring with substantial lags following the return of insurance capacity to the market.

In 1990, the average rate for property insurance in moderate-risk countries in the East Caribbean was 0.4 percent, meaning that for a $100,000 limit on a property the insured would pay $400. Following Hurricane Andrew in 1992, prices surged, reaching 1.3 percent in 1994. Since 1994, the world catastrophe reinsurance market has improved, and rates declined to an estimated 0.70 percent for 1998 and remained so through 1999. What is clear from this, however, is that the price of insurance tripled for property owners in the East Caribbean, without any change in some of the islands' underlying risks. Many countries suffered no hurricane losses over this period. The price fluctuations reflected changes in the supply of catastrophe reinsurance following disasters in Florida and around the world[6]. It also reflected a changed perception by reinsurers on the potential cost of hurricanes. After Hurricane Andrew, insurers increased their estimates of the potential losses from catastrophes by a factor of 3 to 4 times[7]. The figure below not only takes into account the price increases but also the supply shortages which were reflected in higher retentions of risk by the primary insurers.

---

[6] For a more detailed analysis of this 'supply crunch', see Froot, Kenneth, "The Limited Financing of Catastrophic Risk", September 1997; and "The Pricing of U.S. Catastrophe Insurance", March 1997; Harvard Business School and National Bureau of Economic Research. Froot shows how increasing reinsurance prices simultaneous with less coverage purchased, inherently reflects a supply shift with reinsurers reducing the availability of catastrophic coverage.

[7] There was a severe tightening in world catastrophe reinsurance markets following Hurricane Andrew which hit Florida in August 1992 and generated about US$18 billion in insured losses. In 1993, insurance prices were between 5 and 7 times their historical average, however, since 1995 the market has eased, and during the 1997-98 El Niño period, the Atlantic hurricane season was abnormally low due to the stronger northern Jet Stream effect which penetrated further eastward into the Atlantic and prevented usual hurricane formations. However, a renewed hazard event frequency (both in the Caribbean and worldwide) could easily cause a reversion to tight conditions.

Figure 1.2: Global Reinsurance Rates

1989-1998 Price Index

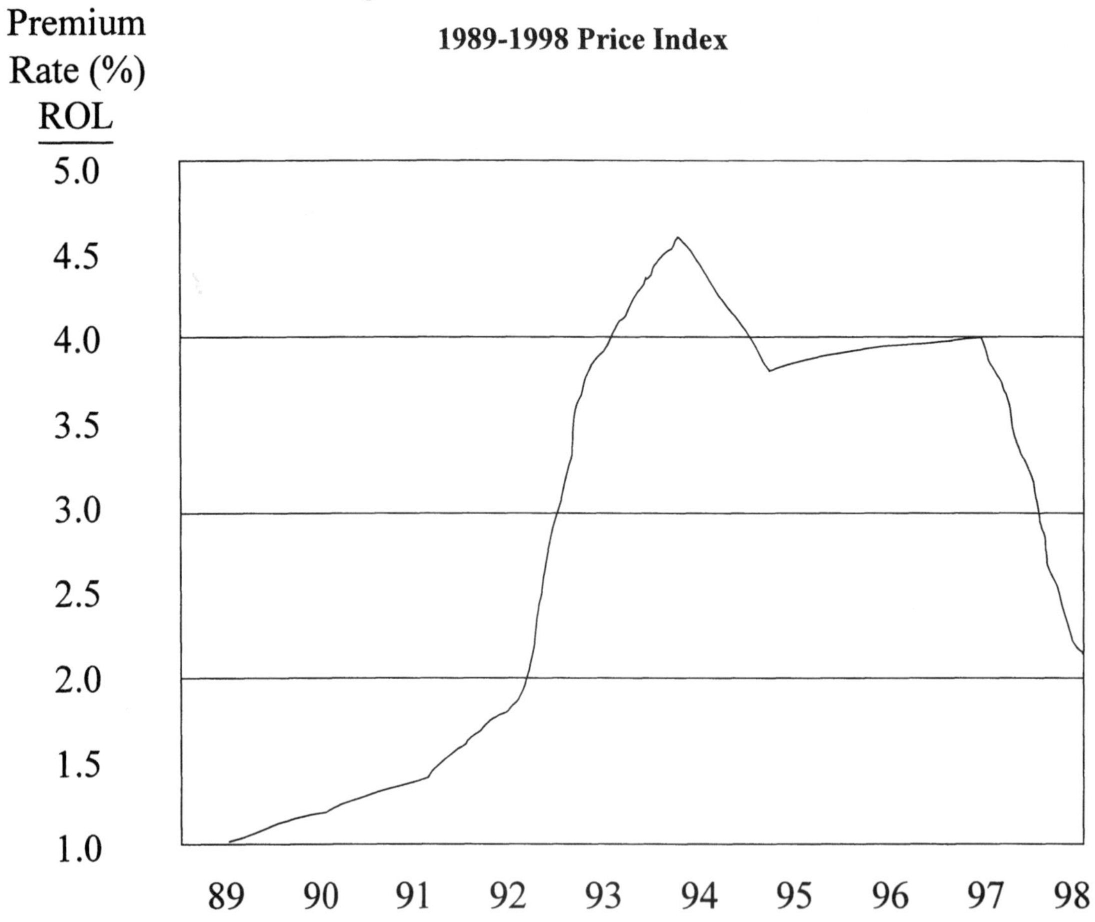

Premium
Rate (%)
ROL

Source: Guy Carpenter.

Figure 1.2 is particularly relevant since direct insurance rates for property in ESC countries are greatly influenced by the cost of reinsurance. In general, over 80 percent of gross written premiums and insurance risks for property, are ceded to reinsurers.

Figure 1.3: Historical Excess of Loss Reinsurance Rates

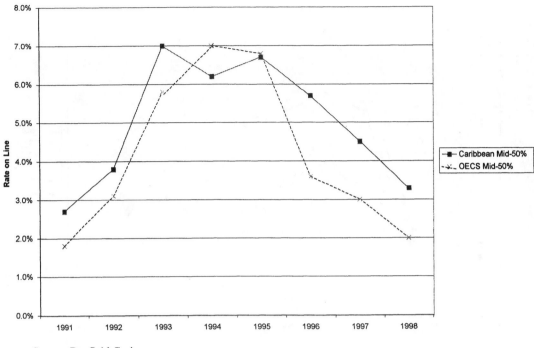

Source: Benfield Greig

Excess of loss reinsurance rates (rates-on-line)[8] followed the same pattern both in the Caribbean as a whole and in the OECS countries as seen in Figure 1.3. High volatility was experienced in excess of loss premiums at the middle (50%) layer of reinsurance cover, that is, at the midpoint in the range of excess-of-loss coverage layers. The period between 1993-95 was the peak with rates on line reaching 7%. At the lower layers of cover which would be accessed more often (e.g.: first 5%), rates were much higher during 1993-95, in some countries reaching up to 16% of loss amounts insured.

---

[8] The term "rate on line" refers to the premium dollar price as a percentage of the loss level (in $ damages) to be covered under an excess of loss contract. In this sense it is akin to cost of capital or the interest cost of capital. Rate on line should not be confused with the premium as a % of total insured value. Since rate on line is the price of compensation for exact losses measured in dollar terms, such loss levels are generally a sub-set of the total insured value (and based on a probabilistic application to expected and maximum losses).

Figure 1.4: Average Caribbean Catastrophe Rates - Commercial Properties

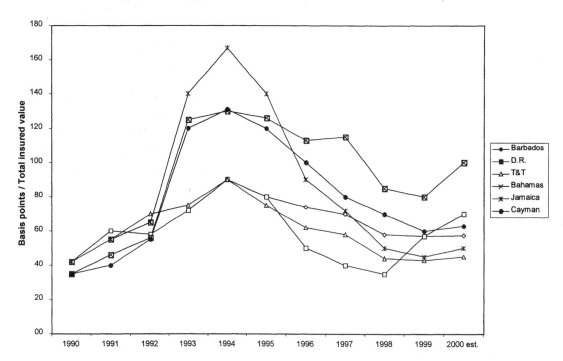

Source: CARICOM Working Party

This pattern was experienced across the wider Caribbean as Figure 1.4 shows for catastrophe primary premium rates on commercial property where volatility was particularly apparent in rates charged in countries such as Jamaica but also Bahamas and Cayman Islands. The volatility parameters are summarized below:

Table 1.2: Volatility Indicators of Global and Caribbean Reinsurance and Primary Insurance Rates

	Global XL Rate Price Index	Carib-bean XL Rates (50% mid-point)	OECS XL Rates (50% mid-point)	Barbados Commer-cial Rates	Domin. Republic Comm. Rates	Trinidad and Tobago Comm. Rates	The Bahamas Comm. Rates	Jamaica Comm. Rates	Cay-man Islands Comm. Rates
Standard Deviation	1.3%	1.6%	2.1%	0.13%	0.17%	0.16%	0.34%	0.45%	0.34%
Rate Mean	2.7%	5.2%	4.4%	0.65%	0.59%	0.6%	0.92%	0.83%	0.79%
Standard Deviation Normalized to Mean	49%	31%	48%	20%	29%	27%	37%	54%	42%

Source: Benfield Greig; CARICOM Working Party

The key indicator to take account is the standard deviation normalized to the mean (coefficient of variation). This shows the actual percentage deviation of the rates from the mean over the period. As can be seen, the global excess-of-loss reinsurance (XL) price index had a percentage standard deviation of 49% around the mean and OECS XL rates were similar at 48%. Primary rates in Jamaica were at record highs showing a percentage standard deviation of 54%, in part due to both the effects of hurricane Andrew in 1992, and previously hurricane Gilbert in 1988 which directly hit Jamaica.

The above analysis shows the large volatility in insurance pricing which affects the Caribbean. Following hurricane Andrew, additional reinsurance capacity was created in the Bermuda market as traditional major reinsurers such as Munich Re exited the Caribbean market and world reinsurance prices increased. This additional capacity along with the global development of capital market instruments such as catastrophe bonds financed in the capital markets, have helped stabilize volatility. Nevertheless, future volatility cannot be ruled out, and even a fraction of that seen in the past would be destabilizing to Caribbean insurance markets and the availability of coverage needed against natural hazards.

Within this context, it is observed that a type of 'contagion' effect occurs globally when major disasters use up significant portions of reinsurer capacity. While this contagion does not occur in the same manner as emerging market jitters occur during economic crises, it has a similar effect and essentially reflects supply constraints which result in higher pricing to reach a new supply/demand equilibrium. Such adjustments are widely recognized by insurers and reinsurers alike, and reflect a 'recovery' effort by both insurance and reinsurance providers for capital lost or depleted due to large events. In this sense, catastrophe reinsurance contains elements of risk financing ('finite insurance') to fund the insured party, with compensatory payback obtained through temporarily higher rates. It is widely stated in the industry, therefore, that due to large catastrophe exposures, the low rates seen in the last two years will not continue.

Figure 1.5: Supply Shift and Demand Effect after Catastrophes

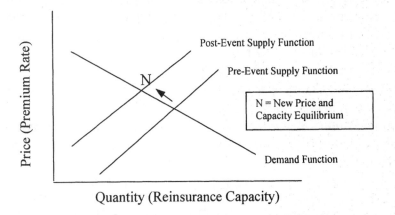

Another factor affecting the stable supply of catastrophe reinsurance relates to the manner in which the market is organized. As expressed in Goldman Sachs' Fixed Income Research on Insurance Linked Securities: "Natural catastrophes such as hurricanes and earthquakes reduce private wealth just as do economic losses on diversified portfolios of stocks and bonds. Nevertheless, a substantial portion of this exposure is borne by private corporations (privately held reinsurance companies) and small numbers of wealthy individuals (Lloyds unincorporated names). This inefficient sharing of risk has resulted in high reinsurance rates and has motivated many primary insurance companies to maintain very large retained exposures and to cease issuing new or renewal policies in selected areas. A more efficient risk sharing procedure would allow the capital markets to spread the risk among large numbers of investors to whom this exposure is a very small portion of their total risk exposure" (Goldman Sachs: Fixed Income Research Series on Insurance Linked Securities).

Professor Kenneth Froot of Harvard University, similarly points out some aspects of these market inefficiencies and why catastrophe risk is distributed inefficiently: "Another reason institutional arrangements may be inefficient is that the lack of objective information acts as a kind of barrier to entry. When objective information is costly to assemble, a greater investment is required to get into the underwriting business. Indeed, when objective information is in short supply, markets tend to be organized around relationships and reputation. By contrast, when objective information is plentiful, markets tend to be organized around transactions, with the players being more interchangeable. Because newcomers are discouraged from entering the market, the incumbents who specialize in underwriting cat risks, such as cat-risk reinsurers, can more easily charge high prices" (The Market for Catastrophic Risk: A Clinical Examination, August 1999).

However, information can be improved through institutional strengthening to increase the collection and dissemination of critical information. In the U.S. for example, the Insurance Services Office enables insurers to achieve and share economies of scale in the collection and analysis of data. Such institutions contribute to improved underwriting and pricing decisions on the part of individual insurers by making pooled data and analyses of pooled data widely available.

Global Reinsurance Capacity and the Caribbean Market

1999 was the third highest loss year in terms of insured losses from catastrophes ($18 billion) with associated economic losses of $80 billion. Similarly, 1998 was the fourth highest loss year in terms of catastrophes causing global insured losses amounting to $15 billion and overall economic losses of $94 billion. This compares to catastrophe insured losses of approximately $27 billion in 1992 and $18.4 billion in 1994, the two years of highest losses to date. Of the $15 billion in losses in 1998, almost 80% were due to windstorm disasters. Catastrophe excess of loss reinsurance cover globally amounted to about $75 billion, and this represented on average, 40% of total coverage with the remainder held by primary insurers or under quota share treaties. The earthquake share of insured and total economic losses in 1999 was substantial, representing over 35% of total losses.

Thus, recent annual losses worldwide averaging around $20 billion would represent about 27% of the current excess of loss capacity and 11% of total available insurance and reinsurance before considering the net surplus capital in the industry. If future windstorms (hurricanes, typhoons, cyclones) increase, or if property affected were in a high value area such as Miami, Florida, there would likely be a squeeze on available reinsurance capacity as additional coverage to protect against large events would reach into the limits of global reinsurance capacity.

While potential devastating events globally could in aggregate cause up to $200 billion in insured losses, this scenario will, statistically speaking not occur in any single year or closely consecutive years. However, because of these constraints and the potential for worldwide catastrophes to significantly 'bite' into the reinsurance market's capacity, the consideration of alternative risk transfer and financing instrument makes sense in the context of providing additional available risk financing via the world's capital markets.

The table below indicates that, in the period following hurricane Andrew, the rates for ESC nations were generally in line or higher than those for Miami, but much higher than the rates for the less hurricane exposed cities of Tampa and Tallahassee. Thus the international insurance pricing equally affected those areas affected by the hurricane (Florida, Bahamas) and those Caribbean countries which were not affected.

Table 1.3: Base Property Rates (on insured value) for ESC Countries Compared with Coastal Areas in the U.S. (1994 - post hurricane Andrew)

ESC and other CARICOM countries	Price in % per $0.1 mn. limit
Antigua	1.10
Bahamas	1.20
Barbados	1.00
Belize	0.90
Dominica	0.90
Grenada	1.02
Montserrat	1.00
St. Kitts and Nevis	0.95
St. Lucia	1.15
St. Vincent	1.05
Trinidad and Tobago	0.77
Turks and Caicos (associate member)	1.11
United States (Florida)	
Miami	0.99
Tampa	0.59
Tallahassee	0.43

Source: Insurance Information Institute (I.I.I.)

The pricing for excess of loss reinsurance, i.e., the rate-on-line, varies by type of risk. A primary company writing in a low catastrophe exposed area will pay the lowest rates on line. Rates also vary by retention level. The rate on line for $15 million in coverage above a retention level of $10 million will be much higher than for $15 million above a $100 million retention level[9]. This is because there is a higher probability of losses exceeding $15 million than exceeding $100 million.

---

[9] Retention level is the insured amount that is 'retained' by the original/primary insurer after it has 'reinsured' or 'ceded' a portion of its portfolio to the reinsurer. In the East Caribbean, primary insurers reinsure on average 80% of their portfolio, thus effectively retaining only 20% as an insurance risk on their books.

Rates on line for ESC countries, vary from 25-30 percent at the lowest levels of retention (with highest exposure and probability) to 2-3 percent at the top levels. An average level would be 9 percent. Retention levels for the ESC countries are much lower on average than for U.S. insurers, but exposure to hazards are higher. Initially this makes sense from the perspective of 'transferring the risk' outside of the affected countries into the international market, however, as the subsequent analysis will show, excessive transfer abroad with very little retention can also be sub-optimal from a cost-effectiveness and risk-sharing point of view.

A different approach to addressing the issue of adequacy of prices is to compare rates on line with "pure" rates developed by models which project hazard frequencies and their intensity in terms of damage functions. This report addresses this issue under the hazard and financial modeling sections. The methodology used for this purpose includes the following steps:

Figure 1.6: Catastrophe Pricing Methodology

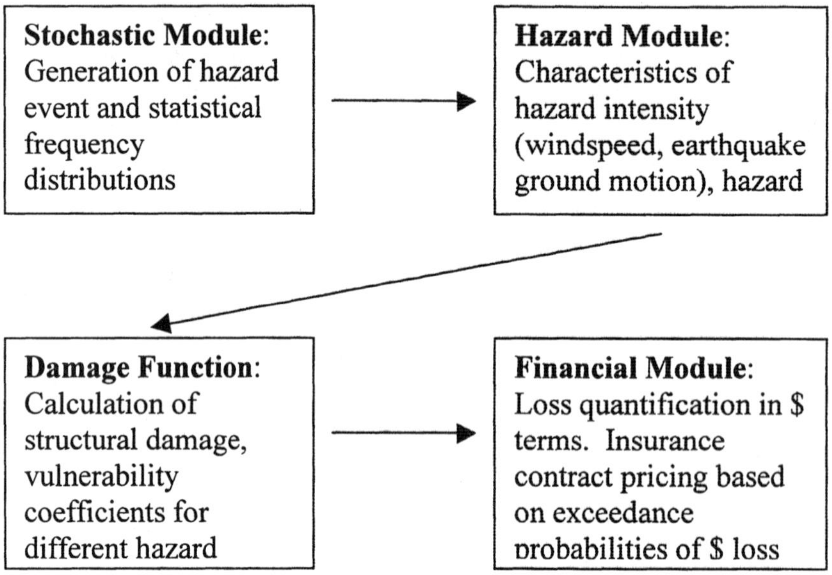

Stochastic Module: Generation of hazard event and statistical frequency distributions

Hazard Module: Characteristics of hazard intensity (windspeed, earthquake ground motion), hazard

Damage Function: Calculation of structural damage, vulnerability coefficients for different hazard

Financial Module: Loss quantification in $ terms. Insurance contract pricing based on exceedance probabilities of $ loss

Under the damage module, a vulnerability function for property structures is established against levels of hazard intensity. This is the 'real sector' input used for subsequent financial modeling for insurance:

Figure 1.7: Structural Vulnerability Function

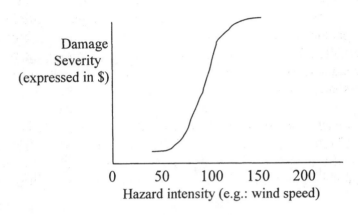

Source: Stubbs, N.; OAS

The above reflects the typical "S" shape damage/severity function for hurricanes. At the lower wind speeds, the damage function increases more slowly in proportion to the increase in wind speed. As the winds surpass 100 mph, the damage level begins increasing proportionately at a higher rate. After reaching top winds, the damage function decreases in its 'acceleration' since the incremental wind speed does little additional damage to the gross destruction already done.

To provide some perspective of the context of this risk market, it is estimated that the ESC countries generate currently about $150 million in insurance premiums. Most ESC countries face a high level of risk. The islands are in the front line of Atlantic storm activity. A number of the islands have significant earthquake risk as well. A few countries have a volcano risk, most notably Montserrat, where an eruption in 1996 caused extensive damage.

Projections by risk management firms show that the East Caribbean region can expect 2.5 storms every year. Severe hurricanes, defined as category 3, 4 and 5, have, up until the late 1990s been less common. Category 3 hurricanes can be expected to occur every second year, and Category 5 storms every fifth year.

Reviewing recent hurricane experience, the following records are obtained:

**Table 1.4: Hurricanes that Affected Caribbean
Countries Between 1970-1999**

Year	Hurricane	Country
1974	Carmen	Jamaica
1974	Fifi	Belize, Jamaica
1979	David	Dominica
1980	Allen	Barbados, St. Lucia, St. Vincent, Jamaica
1984	Klaus	Dominica
1985	Gloria	Antigua, St.Kitts, Turks and Caicos, Anguilla
1987	Emily	Grenada, St. Vincent

1987	Floyd	Bahamas
1988	Gilbert	Dominica, Jamaica, G. Cayman, St. Lucia
1988	Joan	Tobago
1989	Hugo	Antigua, Dominica, Guadeloupe, Montserrat, St. Kitts
1992	Andrew	Bahamas
1994	Debbie	St. Lucia
1995	Iris	Antigua, Dominica, St. Vincent, Trinidad and Tobago
1995	Erin	Bahamas
1995	Marilyn	Dominica
1995	Luis	Anguilla, Antigua, Dominica, Montserrat, St. Kitts and Nevis
1998	Georges	St. Kitts and Nevis, Antigua
1999	Floyd	Bahamas
1999	Jose	St. Kitts, Antigua
1999	Lenny	St. Lucia, Grenada, St. Kitts, Dominica, St. Vincent

Source: Insurance Information Institute

The experience of the twenty-year period, suggests that the Caribbean countries would be damaged by two tropical storms each year and by a hurricane every two years. In general, climatologists view the 1969 to 1989 period as *below* average in terms of cyclonic activity in the Atlantic. So far, nine hurricanes have hit the Caribbean islands in the 1990s, or an average of almost one per year, double the rate of the prior 20 years.

There are significant regional differences in exposure, however. Northern and eastern islands are more exposed than southern islands. The Leeward Islands including Antigua, Montserrat, St. Kitts and Nevis are viewed as being most exposed, while Trinidad and Tobago have minimal exposure.

Insurance loss modeling thus, involves three main steps: An assessment is made of the probability of the underlying natural phenomena, either hurricane storms or earthquakes and their intensities. This information is developed from historical meteorological and seismic data. The second step is to assess the exposure level and vulnerability of insured property to differing hazard intensities (as per the graph above). The third step is to combine the information from the first two steps and produce a probable loss distribution in dollar terms.

To illustrate, consider an extremely simple example of a small island, subject to only a category II type hurricane. The probability of such a hurricane striking the island is 10 percent. In other words, it can be expected that such a hurricane will hit the island once every ten years. The value of insured property on the island is $100 million. It is estimated that a category II storm hitting the island will cause $20 million in insured loss. This information can then be used to calculate appropriate annual insurance rates and to decide on the maximum capital ($20 million) needed in any given year to pay losses.

Insurance loss modeling develops data on these two main figures -- annual average loss and probabilities of maximum losses -- from data on multiple meteorological or seismological events.

The Nature of Catastrophic Risk

Catastrophic risks in primary markets tend to be spread temporally more than spatially. For example, prior to Hurricane Andrew, insurance companies added a 14 percent catastrophic property factor to insurance premiums in Florida. With residential insurance premiums totaling $1.2 billion in 1992, this resulted in the catastrophe portion of premiums of $168 million per year. This factor was based on loss data for 30 to 40 years. The assumption was that catastrophe losses would average out to 14 percent of the premium over 40 years. In any single year, a large hurricane could cause losses many times the $168 million in premium. However, the companies assumed that over a 30 to 40 year period they would break even.

The pricing of catastrophe reinsurance is based on the notion of spreading risk over time. The reinsurance company promises to indemnify the primary company for losses above a retention level. For example, a primary insurance company might purchase reinsurance for catastrophe losses between $20 million and $30 million. In pricing this $10 million layer of insurance, the reinsurer will first estimate the probability of loss in this range. Let us assume that this probability is 10 percent. In other words, the reinsurer believes that once every ten years the primary insurer will need to pay losses of $20 million or more. If the reinsurer charges a rate of 10 percent it will break even over time. This rate is known as the "pure premium". To come up with the final rate, the reinsurer adds a factor for expenses and profit. The final rate is expressed as a percent of the $10 million layer of insurance provided and is called the rate on line, as discussed earlier.

There is a third way that risk is spread by insurance, which is of some relevance to the ESC region. We can label this way as "speculative." Insurance organizations provide insurance for somewhat exotic risks such as satellite launches. The pricing of these risks are calculated on a slim if any actuarial basis and they are not spread over space or time. It could be argued that if enough of these event risks are taken on, they involve a spreading of the risk. In other words, if Lloyd's insures 100 such diverse risks, and by the laws of probability only one of them results in a claim, then the premiums for the 99 are paying for the loss of the one. Some risks in the ESC region could be viewed as falling into this "speculative" category. A reinsurance or insurance company with excess capital might take a risk from the ESC region on a "speculative" basis. The net effect of treating ESC reinsurance risks in this fashion is to create increased volatility in the marketplace. In a period of excess capacity in worldwide reinsurance markets, reinsurance will be readily available to primary companies in the ESC region. In periods of tight capacity, reinsurance will be in short supply.

There is also the danger of a major or even total withdrawal of reinsurance capacity to the region. The state of Hawaii faced this problem following Hurricane Iniki in 1992 and in Fiji in the mid-1980s. Such a withdrawal would have disastrous consequences for the economies concerned. Without insurance, the financing of construction would be greatly diminished. The fact that catastrophe risks are spread over time has two important implications for ESC markets: Reinsurance or risk transfer relationships need to be long-term in nature: Major primary insurers around the world have long-term relationships with their reinsurers. So if a reinsurer has a large loss in a particular year, the "loss" will be made up by payments from the primary company in future years. If reinsurers do not have a long-term relationship then they view a large loss as more in the speculative area where they are making a one-year bet. As a result they will require a higher profit rate for this risk, as has occurred in the ESC region.

Figure 1.8 shows the economic (unsured) losses and insured losses from 1980 to 1999 for weather related disasters, globally. From weather related disasters alone (excluding earthquake), 1998 was the year with the highest total economic losses worldwide. 1999 was the third highest year for total economic losses as well as weather related insured losses. Generally, hurricane and windstorm losses in a given year

Figure 1.8: Insured and Uninsured Losses from Weather Related Natural Disasters

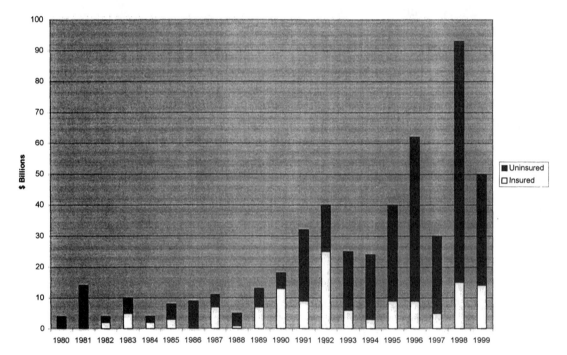

Source: Munich Re; Guy Carpenter

represent about 70% of total losses, however, in 1999, earthquakes represented almost 40% of insured losses from events in Colombia, Turkey, Greece and Taiwan.

1999 was also a year with significant flood damage in Central Europe and South East Asia as well as hailstorms in Australia and gale storms in Europe (Lothar, Martin). Windstorm damages include for the U.S. and the Caribbean those from hurricane Floyd, the Orissa cyclone in India, tropical cyclone Bart in Japan, as well as major tornadoes in Oklahoma. Total economic losses from weather related and earthquake events combined approximated $100 billion in 1999 compared to $93 billion in 1998, and for all events, insured losses were higher in 1999 as well ($22 bn.)compared to 1998. The intensifying loss trends, requiring matching insurance risk capital, can be attributed to increased urbanization, population growth, rising growth of both number and value of properties in catastrophe prone areas, as well as climatological and environmental changes.

Given the context of global disaster risks as well as the risk exposure in the Caribbean, the following chapter examines the operation of the property insurance market in the Caribbean. Based on the nature of catastrophic risk, the organization and structure of the domestic market in the Caribbean represents the first line of defense for successful risk management. The following chapter thus identifies some of the domestic industry and regulatory factors which could constrain effective capacity in the management of such catastrophic risks.

II. THE PROPERTY INSURANCE MARKET IN THE CARIBBEAN

The structure of the Caribbean insurance industry has to-date depended primarily on a strategy of substantial transfer of insurance risks to the international reinsurance markets. While such a strategy has allowed a reduction in financial exposures, it has also reduced the incentives for domestic underwriting and risk management capacities, and has linked the local market development cycle to external market movements. The large number of players in the local domestic markets along with the practice of extremely modest retentions of risk, does not permit sufficient flexibility at the country level to optimize the risk management, risk transfer and premium pricing options in the most cost effective manner. The high vulnerability of individual countries calls for improved risk pooling strategies, some of which have been attempted in limited ways in the past. These can help lower the insurance cycle risk while promoting regulatory changes to both strengthen domestic insurance suppliers and promote improved loss reduction measures.

II. THE PROPERTY INSURANCE MARKET IN THE CARIBBEAN

Large catastrophic events like hurricanes have direct costs as they lead not only to large losses of capital stock and inventories but also indirect costs in lost income, employment or services which result from lost productive capacity. These events jeopardize internal and external macroeconomic stability leading to larger than anticipated public sector and balance of payments deficits. For example, the direct effects of hurricane Gilbert on Jamaica in 1988, amounted to US$956 million representing 27 percent of GDP, with half from losses in agriculture, tourism and industry, 30 percent in housing, and 20 percent in economic infrastructure. As a result of the hurricane, losses in export earnings were estimated at US$130 million representing 14 percent of exports, and the government incurred US$220 million in additional expenditures while the public sector deficit increased from an earlier expected 2.8 percent of GDP to 10.6 percent, also fueling inflation.

While 80% of the gross property insurance premiums are transferred to reinsurers, the actual remittance flow is reduced by the reinsurance commission paid by reinsurers (e.g.: 30% of 80% = 24%). A year with abnormally high property claims experience can of course, result in a net remittance inflow from reinsurers. Tight reinsurance conditions, i.e., a high priced market, can give very good results for well managed Caribbean companies as high reinsurance costs materially boost reinsurance commission incomes. Policy coverage restrictions are generally designed and imposed by foreign reinsurers, and their effect falls on the policyholders rather than on the insurance companies.

Historically, there have been very mixed feelings as to the industry's role for a proactive involvement in promoting hazard and vulnerability mitigation measures. While not denying the inherent benefit of such measures, the insurance companies' concerns center on the implementation complexities and costs, particularly as reinsurers are seen as unlikely to share in these costs. Companies view the leadership role for mitigation measures as lying with their governments.

The insurance markets are intensively competitive for the property insurance classes -- a competition primarily seeking reinsurance commission revenues rather than underwriting, or 'risk taking' profits. The larger Caribbean insurance markets contain insurance companies (with sizeable markets shares), forming part of broader commercial groups. It is estimated, however, that several insurance companies are under capitalized and markets are saturated. New regulations expected to come into effect in Barbados, the OECS and Trinidad and Tobago will significantly increase capital requirements thus likely leading to mergers and buy-outs within the local industry.

Table 2.1: Structure of the East Caribbean General/Property Insurance Market (1998)

	Antigua and Barbuda	Barbados	Dominica	Grenada	St. Kitts and Nevis	St. Lucia	St. Vincent and the Grenadines	Trinidad and Tobago	Total
No. of General Insurance Companies	16	22	13	19	9	21	12	29	141
% Foreign Companies[a]	88%	45%	95%	76%	67%	86%	85%	12%	66%
Property Insurance Premiums (millions)	$ 10.6	$ 43.0	$ 5.8	$ 8.6	$6.3	$11.9	$ 9.6	$ 52.1	$148
Gross Premiums % of GDP	1.8%	3.0%	2.4%	2.7%	2.4%	2.1%	3.3%	0.9%	2.3%

a. Of these, approximately ¾ are companies from Trinidad, Barbados and Guyana.
Source: Eastern Caribbean Central Bank (ECCB)

Table 2.2: Insurance Sector Regulatory Characteristic in the East Caribbean Markets
($US Dollars Equivalent)

	Antigua and Barbuda	Barbados	Dominica	Grenada	St. Kitts and Nevis	St. Lucia	St. Vincent and the Grenadines	Trinidad and Tobago
Minimum Capital Requirement (millions)	$0.07 .	$1.5	$0.07	$0.09	$0.07	Local $0.10m Foreign $0.20m	$0.07	$0.16
Solvency Margin (Assets – Liab.) above premium income	Min. capital or 10 % of prem. income	$0.25 or 25% of premium income	Min. capital or 10 % of prem. income	$0.06m or 10% of prem. Income	Min. capital or 10% of premium income	$0.07m or 20% of premium income	Min. capital. or 10% of premium income	Min. capital. or 20% of premium Income
Reserve Requirement	na	40% of annual premium income	30% annual prem. Income	na	10% of annual premium	40% of annual premium income	na	40% of premium income
Premium tax	na	5%	None	na	5%	Local: 3% foreign: 5%	3%	6%
Corporate tax	40%	40%	30%	30%	38%	33.3%	40%	35%

Na =not available
Source: Eastern Caribbean Central Bank (ECCB)

Observations on East Caribbean Market Characteristics

The proportion of residential and commercial properties in the Caribbean covered by insurance is significantly higher than in most developing countries, on account of both the susceptibility to natural disasters but also on the influence of tourism and the requisite insurance of tourist facilities. In comparison with the insurance density in the U.S. (3.3% of GDP for the property and casualty business), the average for the OECS, Barbados and Trinidad and Tobago is 2.3% of the combined countries' GDP.

The number of general/property insurance companies in the East Caribbean, however, is large. The ratio of premiums earned ($149 mn.) to number of primary companies writing property business (numbering 145) is just a little over $1 million, i.e., the average premium written per company. In contrast, the average premium written per company in the U.S. (2,500 companies in total), is $112 million or a multiple of one hundred times that of the East Caribbean. However, such a comparison may not be necessarily meaningful given the different levels of development and insurance markets. Nevertheless, if one takes the relative populations serviced by insurance companies, the results are:14,000 inhabitants are served per each insurance company in the East Caribbean versus 107,000 inhabitants in the U.S. served per each company. This would suggest a potentially over extended industry in the East Caribbean which implies inefficiencies of scale in terms of both operating costs and risk management. A significant share of companies, however, effectively function as agencies with little desire to operate as genuine risk underwriters.

While most of the East Caribbean countries do not admit non-registered insurance companies, the actual insured base in each country is likely higher than reported due to non-admitted providers. In those countries where non-registered companies are allowed to conduct business, large commercial and tourist properties are directly insured abroad. Due to the non-reporting nature of these businesses at the Caribbean level, figures on this market are difficult to estimate although via the tallying of the total market value of insurable assets and comparison of these with the premiums collected annually, one could, by process of elimination deduce the quantity of assets insured directly abroad.

On average, 75% of the OECS market is held by Trinidadian and Barbadian companies. Thus, the East Caribbean insurance market (prior to reinsurance) is effectively a Barbados and Trinidad dominated market.

Regulatory Developments

Solvency margin regulations generally follow the EU regulatory systems whereby such margins are indicated by capital requirements of at least 20% of premium income. In Trinidad and Tobago, features of the Canadian system were adopted. However, new Canadian norms recently developed, include additional safeguards such as the provision for catastrophe reserving for earthquakes, a practice which would equally apply to the hurricane and wind storm risks in the Caribbean.

Expense ratios in the Caribbean are relatively high, between 30%-40% of premium income compared to the U.S. average expense ratio of between 26%-28%. Expense ratios reflect the costs of business acquisition, brokerage fees, underwriting fees, administrative costs and overhead as a percentage of annual premiums earned. In the Caribbean, due to the relatively small size of companies and diseconomies of scale, expense ratios constitute a higher percentage of annual premium income, despite the fact that administrative and staff costs are generally lower than in the U.S. Such costs as well as low retentions of underwriting risks prevent a quicker build up of capital reserves/surplus, than could otherwise be achieved.

A new OECS Insurance Act is under review by those member governments, and this would substantially raise minimum capital requirements as in Trinidad. In Trinidad and Tobago, the minimum capital requirement will be changed to $1.6 million to be phased in within 5 years. The new OECS Act would require minimum capital of $0.9 million for local companies and a requirement of $1.8 for foreign companies. The differentiation is meant to provide a competitive adaptation period for indigenous companies to reduce costs and increase their scale economies, and for foreign companies, to ensure that sufficient capital for operations and claims settlement, is maintained. In Grenada and St. Lucia existing regulations already provide for differentiated capital requirements for foreign companies. The new Insurance legislation, however, will attempt to harmonize the regulatory requirements across all of the OECS to include uniform solvency margins (e.g.: 20% of premium).

In OECS countries, all insurers must be registered locally whether foreign or domestic. In contrast, Barbados and T&T have separate regulations for non-registered foreign companies, although there is concern about monitoring such business more carefully given the non-reporting of such entities.

In terms of exchange controls, approval by most central banks is required for transfers above specified level (as in the banking sector) and in some cases, a remittance charge of 1% is applied to premiums ceded to reinsurers. However, these regulations are being relaxed in line with WTO standards, and thresholds requiring approval are being increased.

Reserve requirements are generally high and require prescribed investments of surplus of companies, a factor which might reduce overall profitability if other more high yielding investment opportunities become available. Premium (sales) taxes, corporate taxes, and stamp taxes vary widely across the East Caribbean – factors which also will require harmonization if further market integration and pooling structures are to be considered.

Catastrophe Insurance Reserves

Insurance company reserves fall into two basic categories. First are the shareholders' capital and free 'surplus' reserves, and second, the insurance or 'technical' reserves. The latter are customarily tax deductible being constituted for known liabilities such as payment of reported but unpaid claims and the unexpired portion of pre-paid, (e.g. annual), premiums. In effect, the capital and free reserves represent the solvency margin and are intended as the last asset resource should the technical reserves prove inadequate.

Relating these considerations to natural hazard peril insurance, there are two particular factors. First, although catastrophes are accepted as severe but infrequent events, in accounting terms (Generally Accepted Accounting Principles - GAAP), they cannot be precisely forecasted as to timing or amount. Secondly, over 80% of the insured catastrophe liabilities fall under reinsurance contracts placed mostly outside the Caribbean. These two factors prompt a local insurer to first determine how to prudently reserve for the net liability retention (approximately 20%) before the catastrophe event occurs, and second how to ensure that the reinsurers are financially secure enough to meet their liabilities fully and on time for the lion's share (over 80%) of the liabilities.

On the first challenge, Caribbean insurers were, until recently, discouraged by existing tax laws to have incentives to set up specific reserve provisions for catastrophe perils *before* a catastrophe event. Several Caribbean countries are now permitting tax deductibility for such dedicated reserves. Without this dispensation, very little of premium paid becomes available to meet future catastrophe claims liabilities under issued policies. In the absence of a natural hazard event, less than 20% of premiums customarily see their way to increasing free reserves. Operating expenses can characteristically consume 40% of premiums, income tax about 35%, and a 40% dividend policy on the remainder would use up a further 10 %, thereby leaving approximately 15% passing on to free reserves. Hence, in the policyholder's interest, there should be allowed dedicated, properly monitored, tax deductible catastrophe reserves.

Some larger and special risk categories (e.g.: power utilities), have also over recent years found it impossible to obtain full, and in some cases, any, affordable insurance. On occasions such risks have voluntarily devised very high self-insured deductible levels aimed to cover the expected loss damage potential and separate self-insurance funding for business interruption. These risk management arrangements have served to attract greater levels of insurance/reinsurance cover for the higher, less exposed, risk levels. Furthermore, the insurance cost and availability difficulties have prompted trade associations (e.g. Caribbean Hotel Association - CHA), to employ risk management techniques and/or off-shore captive insurance company arrangements to buy reinsurance on a group basis.

A catastrophe insurer's gross potential liabilities (potential losses on sums insured under natural hazard peril policies), can run into hundreds of millions, if not billions of dollars. The gross liabilities are reducible to net liabilities though reinsurance. Provision also needs to be made for so called second event 'reinstatement' scenarios as reinsurance contracts customarily vary from the primary policies' provisions by limitations on protection amounts available for second (and subsequent) catastrophe occurrences during any one reinsurance contract period. At present, a majority of primary insurers' reinsurance contracts cover second event catastrophe losses.

Clearly, a company's capital and free reserves, plus any dedicated catastrophe reserves (and corresponding assets), need to be readily realizable for these purposes. The assets held to cover a company's insurance or 'technical' reserves should not be considered as available for catastrophe claim payment purposes as these technical liability reserves are constituted for their own specific purposes - customarily to cover prior known reported outstanding claims and the unexpired portion of pre-paid (e.g. annual) premiums. These observations argue for an insurance company's capital and free reserves plus any dedicated catastrophe reserves, to be seen as strong enough, and readily available to meet rationally estimated net of reinsurance catastrophe liabilities. The sections that follow also show how the pooling of catastrophe risks also improve the efficient frontier for a more optimal capital/exposure ratio.

An insurance company's investment policy should also select investment instruments which best meet the purposes for which policyholders purchased their insurance, i.e., the invested funds be secure and available for meeting aggregated claims at unknown future dates. One consideration has to be the secondary potential of natural hazard events to adversely affect local financial markets at the time asset realization is required. Specific regulations should support the view that preferred instruments are found in hard currency financial markets least likely to be impacted by natural catastrophes. Likewise, instruments should be placed in open financial markets entirely on an 'arm's length' basis (without any strings attached as opposed to some existing regulations which allow up to 20% of assets being held in intra-industry group holdings).

Regulatory Improvements and Mitigation of Financial Risks

The catastrophe insurance market has a parallel with the overall financial services regulation, whereby the 'hazard' to be mitigated may be a liquidity crunch with a potential for a run on a banking system. A natural hazard could provoke a run on an insurance system. Contagion effects, albeit for different reasons, can occur, and in the insurance case this is particularly evident following catastrophes wherein supply of capital has been compromised and demand for coverage surges. In both the banking and insurance examples, there is the potential for a secondary 'hazard' of public recriminations if the regulatory performance before the event is perceived inadequate.

Development of strong effective and harmonized insurance regulation, therefore, is recommended to include:

- minimum capitalization requirements for local carriers and brokers.
- solvency and liquidity levels, and adequacy of technical reserves.
- adequate asset/liability management (including maturity and currency matching where applicable), as well as reinsurance credit risk.
- incentives and requirements (including tax concessions) to build-up catastrophic reserve funds up to minimum required levels.
- minimum standards for non-ceded retention of local coverage.
- accurate verification and valuation of companies' balance sheet entries to ensure adequate financial capacity to cover claims.
- increased allowance for overseas investments of insurance assets.
- industry entry requirements including admission of suitable foreign competitors.
- requirements to verify security and reliability of overseas reinsurers who take on portfolios of local coverage.
- linkage of insurance regulation to building code compliance prior to providing insurance coverage, or to discounts based on vulnerability reduction measures.
- monitoring and inspection techniques.
- conditions for revoking licenses and shutting down operations.
- consolidated regional and institutional harmonization of regulators/supervisors.

Recent Limited-Basis Pooling Initiatives

For the most part, government physical assets such as buildings, schools, libraries, roads, and some hospitals are uninsured or underinsured. Exceptions include Barbados with the government owned Insurance Corporation of Barbados responsible for insuring public assets. Additional exceptions include properties owned by statutory corporations such as port and airport authorities, as well as utility companies that can independently access the insurance markets.

Utility companies in particular, to reduce insurance cost, have been actively considering a regional self-insurance program with the Caribbean Development Bank (CDB) and the Caribbean Electric Utilities Service Corporation (CARILEC). Although in the conceptual stage, the program's principal concepts include a backstop credit line in the initial years of premium accumulation. As the fund grows, the utility companies should rely less on the line of credit until it eventually becomes a standby support to be used only after the fund is depleted because of claims arising from a catastrophe event at the uppermost loss levels.

The Barbados Light and Power Company Limited (BLP) started its own self insurance program, due to unavailability of Transmission and Distribution (T and D) catastrophe insurance coverage in 1993, and the subsequent extraordinary high rates to obtain the coverage, estimated at 25% of the estimated losses of assets in a catastrophic event. The fund is composed of cash and committed lines of credit. Similar to the regional approach, the lines of credit are to be used only after the cash portion of the fund is depleted. BLP is now able to look at its insurance needs from a more reasonably priced excess of loss layer, above the level of its self-insurance fund. The company estimates very significant annual premium cost savings.

In 1993, The Caribbean Hotel Association (CHA) retained a US-based risk management firm to perform a pan-Caribbean study regarding wind storm risks to its members' properties to see if there was some way of reducing the upward spiraling costs of insurance. The computer-generated wind study performed by a sub-contractor of the risk management firm provided a probable maximum loss profile of the region and divided the Caribbean into 6 different risk zones. The study suggested that there appeared to be enough diversification of risks among these zones to allow a regional insurance company for the CHA properties to survive a 1.3% probability of a major storm disaster event. Using the expected loss (EPL) information as the starting point, and based on their own financial modeling capabilities, the risk management firm determined a capitalization figure for a regional insurance company to sell 'all risks' property insurance to each of the 1,000 CHA or so members. The risk management firm then created, and today manages a Bermuda insurance company whose exclusive clientele are members of the CHA.

Incentives and Disincentives to Risk-Based Pricing

For many homeowners, the answer to soaring insurance rates, during the 3 years following 1992, was to reduce or eliminate their coverage. With the lack of statistics, it is difficult to measure the degree to which capital stocks are underinsured though 30% is estimated in the insurable housing sector and in most ESC countries few government assets and buildings are insured. From an insurance industry perspective, underinsurance is business lost which would otherwise carry little incremental acquisition cost. Furthermore, policyholders who terminate their insurance seldom return. Insurance, is a discretionary expense, and once terminated, becomes excluded from buying patterns. Local governments are, of course, concerned since the greater the non-insurance (or underinsurance) by a population, the longer it takes for the local economy to recover from catastrophic events.

Two local trends, as yet slowly evolving, may suggest some change in strategy in the markets. First is the setting up of tax deductible dedicated catastrophic reserve funds by a few insurers. This, at current understood levels, will take a long time to justify reduced reliance on reinsurance. Second, there is some increase in the buying of 'excess of loss' reinsurance versus the traditional 'proportional' or 'quota share' reinsurance. The former is perceived more costly up front, making this strategy affordable only for the financially stronger companies, however, its use can permit better risk management and accumulation of capital for well managed companies. Further trends include several nations' regulatory reforms which embrace very much needed increased minimum capital requirements and tighter solvency ratios for insurance companies.

Regrettably, from an overall disaster mitigation standpoint, there has existed for Caribbean catastrophe insurance companies a strong economic rationale inhibiting the spread of vulnerability reduction measures via insurance incentives. As earlier discussed, blanket reinsurance pricing across a whole portfolio works against encouraging insurance companies' adoption of individual risk discriminatory premium pricing. This argument, on the surface, is valid and is exacerbated by the market's fierce competition for reinsurance commission revenues.

Insurance companies therefore have perceived that their primacy lies in obeying the reinsurers' imposed broad pricing methodology and defending their reinsurance commission revenues. They fear that significant premium discounts for the better protected risks (however well merited), cannot be balanced by surcharging the poorer risks and they would end up paying the shortfall in reinsurance premium from their own pockets. Given that characteristically the reinsurers' share of catastrophe policies' premiums exceeds 80%, one can appreciate the basis of insurers' attitudes. One could argue that an insurance company should be better off with a portfolio of the better risks, to which discounts had been awarded and would result in fewer claims -- this argument, however, has little acceptance because such a strategy would imply loss of the reinsurance commission from the poorer risks no longer insured. This is not, however, necessarily seen as an incentive to reinsurers who take on the bulk of overall catastrophe liabilities, i.e., both the good and poorer risks, since it would imply closer and better monitoring costs, and more highly differentiated risk pricing.

In addition, Caribbean primary insurer attitudes were also influenced until some 3 years ago by the earlier tariff market mechanisms which worked to limit price competition. One particular segment of the insurance industry, however, has for over a century been practicing vulnerability reduction as part of its underwriting practices: insurance companies participating in the Factory Mutual (FM) system and the Industrial Risks Insurers (IRI) consortia based in the U.S. impose stringent design criteria and supervise construction as preconditions for underwriting a property. As a consequence, participating companies, some of which have had links to business in the Caribbean, have a much better understanding of the true risk to which a property is subject and are able to offer much lower premiums than traditional insurance companies.

However, as mentioned, the two inhibitors to encouraging vulnerability reduction measures via premium incentives suffer themselves from being non-discriminatory from a reinsurer's standpoint. Both the blanket portfolio reinsurance premium rate and the reinsurance commission being commonly priced on all ceded premiums do little to promote overall risk quality in a reinsurer's accepted portfolio of risks. There are some profit commission arrangements, very limited for 'catastrophe' reinsurance specifically, whereby the earned reinsurance commission rate varies by the loss ratio experienced - i.e. from the claims incurred. Such arrangements still, do not directly address portfolio risk quality improvement.

The adaptation of the working of reinsurance premium pricing and reinsurance commission mechanisms is feasible to meet the objective of encouraging improvement in risk quality of portfolios and hence allowing discriminatory premium pricing for vulnerability reduction measures by policy holders. What is first required is a set of meaningful and workable risk quality criteria mutually agreed by an insurance company and reinsurers. The implementation of risk-based premium pricing, to be successful, would therefore require a comprehensive hazard mapping effort, the inventorying of all typologies of structures and contents with respect to vulnerability, and certification by engineers of individual risk characteristics. Coupled with the actuarial estimates of event probabilities and intensities, and identifying market values which can be used to calculate probable losses, such an exercise would thus set the base for a more accurate catastrophe risk accounting methodology in the Caribbean insurance industry. This would include classifications of :

- Hazard mapped locations.
- Building type and structure vulnerability characteristics.
- The same as above for building contents.
- Engineering certification for individual risk characteristics (needed to retain discipline and deter discounts being given for 'sales' reasons).
- Application of the above to actuarial/statistical distributions of event probabilities and intensities.
- Determination of fair market value of properties to combine the above factors in establishing expected loss amounts.

To implement such a process which reflects preconditions for improvements in the insurance markets, it is recommended that a Caribbean privately funded insurance services office be established. Such an institution which could operate at a regional or sub-regional level, would be well positioned to develop insurance plans by asset class and advise on prospective loss costs taking into account individual risk characteristics. This would permit primary insurers, at their option, to use such standardized class plans and loss costs in pricing their products. At the request of insurers, such an office would also provide reinsurers with pertinent data which could facilitate the negotiation of reinsurance contracts. Additionally, functions such as inspections of individual properties would be conducted when requested by individual insurers. A key function would also be to maintain updated insurance and risk data on the local industry.

Factors Affecting Catastrophe Insurance Demand

Insurance policies cover the 'natural' catastrophe perils of earthquake, volcano and storm; the last embraces declared hurricanes (>75 mph sustained winds), windstorm, flood and storm surge. Volcano and flood cover is practically unattainable in some areas recognized as particularly prone to these events (e.g.: Montserrat).

Since the late 1980s, full value coverage for catastrophe perils is generally limited by claims deductibles expressed as percentages of the full insurable values. For earthquake these deductibles are characteristically 5% and for hurricane 2%. Soft market conditions in some limited areas have reduced the latter to 1%.

The impact of claims deductibles can be severe to policyholders. As an example, a dwelling valued at $100,000 would only recover above the $2,000 deductible. This amount can be sufficient to meet repair costs for characteristic partial roof damage but a very material amount when related to average disposable income levels.

Policy conditions also provide for the amount of claim to be reduced to the extent the amount of insurance purchased (sum insured) is less than the full insurable value at the time of loss (the 'average clause'). Some variations of this exist, e.g., the adjustment is only made if the policy sum insured is less than 85% of the full market value. Policyholders in Caribbean nations with weak currencies and/or high inflation are especially vulnerable to these provisions.

Socioeconomic and behavioral factors also merit consideration on both the supply and the demand sides of the catastrophe insurance market and it is helpful to segment property assets into their ownership classes:

Private Dwellings   Small/Indigenous, Medium, Large

Private Businesses   Small/Informal, Medium, Large

Public Ownership   Building Structures, Utilities, Public Infrastructures

With regard to private dwellings and business properties, the owners' disposable income levels comprise an important factor in the demand for catastrophe insurance the annual cost of which is near 1% of a structure's value. This substantiates the observation that the small/informal sectors only purchase catastrophe insurance to the extent of lending institutions' requirements (and these can be limited to the amount of outstanding loan principal balances). It is estimated that between 25% and 40% of dwelling stock is uninsured with the small/indigenous segment being the least insured. Furthermore, insurance premiums are higher (less affordable) in areas such as the OECS Leeward islands which suffer frequent storm events.

Medium and large dwelling owners, without the same affordability constraints almost universally carry catastrophe insurance, as is the case with medium and large business property owners. In the case of the latter, business interruption insurance (stoppage as a consequence of catastrophe perils), is seldom purchased although this could mitigate employers' loss of income and employees' loss of pay while a workplace was idle. Larger businesses especially have access to insurance brokers (as opposed to insurance companies' own agents), who are adept at placing covers with 'foreign' insurance companies, i.e., operating without local registration, characteristically from the U.S. or Europe. Such arrangements are especially prevalent in those Caribbean nations where foreign currency is readily accessible for premium remittances.

Given that small property owner segments in the less advantaged sectors do not partake of insurance coverage, it is interesting to note that the Barbados government recently created the Poverty Alleviation Fund under the responsibility of the Minister of Social Transformation. In concept this could perhaps serve as an agency for simple building structure vulnerability reduction measures being implemented (possibly with hands-on assistance from Defense Force members). To some small dwelling and business property owners, traditional insurance is a little understood or respected mechanism. For these sectors, a non-traditional approach via the property tax mechanism could offer a worthwhile level of pre-event risk funding. Simultaneously, governments as a matter of ongoing policy should undertake public education programs and publicity on risk management and the prudent use of insurance for protection.

A modest property tax surcharge could fund a flat amount for storm damage essential repair costs (possibly geared to property square footage). Access to the program could be conditioned on property owners' compliance with elemental storm protection measures (e.g., roof straps), the materials for which could be provided for free. A side effect would be that the arrangement, being independent of the catastrophe insurance market mechanism, would not disturb the available market levels of insurance or reinsurance capacity. As illustrated in the subsequent sections of this report, a sub-regional insurance pool might accumulate surplus capital out of which periodic limited 'dividends' could be paid out to support complementary financing for repair costs in the above mentioned sectors which are generally 'uninsurable' from the industry's standpoint.

This concept would appear to very directly address, at modest cost, the goals of actualizing vulnerability reduction measures and providing pre-event funding for essential repairs. Accomplishments towards these combined goals would diminish both the direct and indirect socioeconomic consequences of storm events. Such a program could also be enabled by a stand-by credit arrangement from an international funding agency as already exists for the OECS countries at the country level[10].

Competitiveness of the Industry

Most of the indigenous/local insurance companies originated some 30 years ago, hitherto having operated as general agencies or branches of foreign (mainly U.K.) insurers. For the most part, local companies continue to day as insurance units of trading and financial companies whose profit strategies center on their role as agents for a wide range of products and services.

The primary classes of insurer transact catastrophe insurance (as opposed to reinsurance) in the Caribbean are:

- *Locally Registered Insurance Companies* regulated by the insurance supervisors of each nation.

- *Regional Insurance Companies* registered in each home country but also conducting business in other Caribbean countries in which they operate.

---

[10] OECS Emergency Recovery and Disaster Management Program, funded by IBRD/IDA to undertake mitigation investments, post emergency reconstruction investments, and institutional disaster preparedness.

- *'Foreign' Insurance Companies* – so called because they are regulated and based outside the Caribbean, mainly in Europe and U.S.A.

It is estimated that the first two have the large preponderance of small and mid-sized dwelling and commercial business; while the latter has a significant and growing share of the larger commercial risks segment. Of the 'foreign' companies, several are exempted from most local regulation and taxation. Bermuda and Barbados are the largest centers for exempt companies.

World Trade Organization developments and CARICOM trade liberalization generally are progressively blurring the original demarcations between the three primary categories of insurer. Today, foreign companies have little practical difficulty in accessing the business they want in nations with reasonable access to strong currencies. They can either issue a 'foreign' policy (e.g. from the US, Canada, or UK), or they can make a 'fronting' arrangement with a local company under which almost all the risk bearing is reinsured back. The selection of method employed generally depends on the relative ease and cost of purchasing foreign currency for premium payment.

Foreign companies are adept at merging Caribbean risks into multinational package programs especially for Caribbean subsidiary operations of multi-national corporations. Foreign companies tailor-make policy coverage and insuring large structures often using insurance risk management techniques seldom encountered in local Caribbean markets. The larger local companies realize the need to compete on technique as well as price but can be deterred from such initiatives because of the relative rigidity of their reinsurance programs which are primarily geared to run-of-the mill heterogeneous small and mid-sized risks. Most local companies' strategies are primarily geared to generating the normally higher margin reinsurance commission levels available from their conventional insuring practices. Foreign insurers, on the other hand, primarily seek profit from their individual risk underwriting expertise acknowledging that expense elements of the premium need to always be kept competitively low.

The practice of insurance in the Caribbean is advanced in comparison to most emerging economies and this most likely reflects the recognized exposure to natural hazards as well as the influx of the tourism industry which demands insurance services to protect its capital investments. However, the local insurance industry, while effective in transferring risks, requires needed improvements in risk underwriting and the ensuing ability to discriminate between risk ratings of property risks to encourage pre-insurance loss mitigation measures. These will, in the long run reduce the costs of insurance for both recipients and suppliers. The next chapter discusses methods whereby local insurers, policyholders, property owners and governments can significantly lower the overall price of insurance, and therefore increase competitiveness through physical vulnerability reduction measures. Such actions should represent a basic underlying strategy for reducing risk in disaster prone regions.

III. MITIGATION, SELF INSURANCE AND VULNERABILITY REDUCTION MEASURES

The natural risk exposure of Caribbean economies implies that even while exploiting the insurance mechanism in the most cost effective manner, this will still result in higher relative premiums compared to other regions in the world. Besides the advantages of risk pooling (discussed in chapter VI) which allows diversification of risk and better leverages the available capital, another major source of both premium and risk reduction, consists of physical measures to reduce the structural vulnerability of properties and critical assets. This chapter shows how very modest investments in mitigation such as roof straps to protect against hurricane force winds can reduce the loss exposure substantially, sometimes by as much as 50%. Such measures need to be accompanied by regulatory enforcement of building codes as well as insurance-based incentives which can be achieved through the standardization of data on construction code ratings and property risk characteristics. These resources can also be harnessed to develop publicly sponsored quasi insurance schemes for vulnerable low income communities, in order to instill a framework and awareness regarding the costs and benefits of both physical and financial risk management tools.

III. MITIGATION, SELF INSURANCE AND VULNERABILITY REDUCTION MEASURES

While the insurance mechanism can be considered a strategic financial instrument for transferring risks which are too intense to bear by individual property holders, both public and private sector, the insurance tool should be used only once all other 'manageable' mitigation measures have been exhausted. As confirmed in the section below, the manageable part of the risk, which can be reduced via physical measures has a great potential for reducing the underlying structural risk of physical assets, with the ensuing effect of dramatically reducing the potential 'loss value' of properties at risk. This in turn has the benefits of commanding lower premiums for such exposures for whose residual non-manageable risks should be transferred via the insurance market. The specifics of such measures are discussed in this section, as well as the hazard information requirements needed to establish the underlying date for classifying insurance risks properly. In addition, these concepts are also applied to managing risks for low income communities where a policy of explicit but limited government insurance can be coupled with mitigation activities that begin 'transferring' such risks away from the public sector.

The mitigation of catastrophe loss (direct loss, ensuing reconstruction debt, and other adverse consequences) includes the following strategies which can reduce structural and financial vulnerability under pooled or non-pooled insurance arrangements:

- Vulnerability Reduction Physical Measures.
- Use of Building Codes and Other Regulatory Measures.
- Generation and Availability of Information on Hazards, Vulnerability and Risk.
- The Contributions of the Insurance Industry.

Vulnerability reduction measures are broadly accepted as the highest-impact mechanisms to reduce catastrophe loss as they operate before the event to neutralize the impact of physical forces. The insurance mechanism, on the other hand, is limited to providing monetary compensation after loss has been incurred. Furthermore, only part of the insurance premium dollar is available to compensate losses as over half is customarily consumed by operating expenses and taxes. The dollar expended on vulnerability reduction (e.g. roof strap retrofitting) retains a very lasting physical protection value.

Empirical data showing vulnerability reduction cost/benefit yield potential is not maintained. However, regional civil engineering experts estimate that on average, expending 1% of a structure's value on vulnerability reduction measures can characteristically reduce the probable maximum loss (PML)[11] from windstorm (CAT III,

---

[11] PML differs from EPL in that PML reflects an estimated 'maximum' loss from an event with a specified intensity and estimated probability, and which is used as a 'reference' benchmark to calculate insurance capital requirements and potential losses within a reasonable time frame. EPL on the other hand, reflects the mean expected loss over a range of events and frequencies. In this regard, PML can be seen as identifying a 'tail' on the loss distribution function which is considered the reference point at which insurers and property owners may consider the need for undertaking preventive risk management actions and holding sufficient capital reserves to cover such an eventuality.

120 mph+) by at least a third. For example a $100,000 dwelling's pre-retrofitting PML of $10,000 would become $3,000 after retrofitting. Such retrofitting is customarily focused on roofs, openings and claddings and often capable of effective installation by a property owner. Similarly, it was reported from Trinidad that relatively simple measures (tying walls to foundations, walls to walls, walls to roof supports, and roof supports to roof sheeting), provide effective structural cohesion to withstand high winds and flash flooding.

Past hurricanes illustrate all too well the cost of indifference to vulnerability reduction measures. Nearly a third of the 1988 Jamaica hurricane Gilbert direct losses (totaling $956 million) were from dwellings primarily caused by the loss of roofs; most of which would have been prevented by effective and inexpensive roof strapping. Hurricane Andrew in 1992 severely ravaged dwellings in Florida as a result of construction code violations, shoddy workmanship, and inadequate inspection enforcement.

International aid and development funding agencies, besides sharing consternation at delays, disruptions, and increased costs, have the strong view that wisely planned hazard and vulnerability reduction efforts and funding before a catastrophe pay excellent dividends in reducing economic impacts. Mitigation expenditures are a very small fraction of the funds spent on reconstruction in the aftermath of catastrophes.

The use of building codes and other regulatory measures capable of encouraging mitigation can be divided into two categories:

Non-Structural:	Identification of hazard-prone areas and limitations on their use
	Land-use allocation and control
	Incentives
Structural:	Use of building codes and materials specifications
	Retrofitting existing structures
	Use of protective devices.

Non-Structural / Regulatory / Risk Rating Measures

Non-structural measures in the Caribbean are in use but on a very limited basis. Hazard mapping, although resource and time intensive, has to be considered the fundamental underpinning of any meaningful strategy for catastrophe mitigation. Hazard mapping in particular has critical application to a rational catastrophe insurance market mechanism and hence to rational reinsurance pooling arrangements. To set the base for providing reliable planning information, governments of the Caribbean should consider as a priority, the mapping of hazard locations (and appropriate zoning regulations) throughout each country, and the inventorying of all properties and physical assets (including building code classifications) to be reflected on such maps and information databases. Such measures not only serve for hazard planning purposes, but also provide the actuarial basis for localized insurance pricing of assets in all zones.

The establishment of comprehensive 'risk data' information bases, also permits the insurance industry to participate in loss mitigation incentives by providing tools to better understand and price local risks. Such information allows taking into account detailed characteristics such as building code ratings when determining potential loss costs to be used in rating insurance coverage for individual properties. This results not only in fairer prices for insurance but also provides an economic incentive for communities to strengthen their building codes and enforcement.

Insurers can take a number of steps to help promote investment in vulnerability mitigation measures and to reduce potential loss profiles on underwritten risks. For this purpose, industry service functions could be established under a specialized industry sponsored office (similar to the Insurance Services Office in the U.S.), in order to assign 'grades' to communities based on the quality of their building codes and their enforcement. For this, a grading schedule reflecting building code enforcement can be established for qualifying communities which may be eligible for premium discounts. Under such a program, grades would be assigned to local communities based on structural factors as well as public protection services (e.g.: disaster preparedness, fire fighting capability, etc.) available. Loss cost estimation and associated premium levels should, in addition to the above factors, be also based on the characteristics of individual properties including location and risk exposure in accordance with the hazard mapping information discussed above.

Structural Measures

Structural measures have also made but limited headway in the Caribbean. The Caribbean Unified Building Code (CUBIC) has now progressed into useable codes in several nations but, as was recently observed, these improved codes lack any effective enforcement practices. Limited progress on retrofitting can be attributed primarily to the lack of incentives and concerted leadership in the promotion of benefit features and practices.

A fee based approach which might result in more effective enforcement actions would be to set up a Bureau de Controle type firm at the regional level, with the responsibility to inspect building during the construction cycle. While political decisions would need to be made to permit such an entity to operate as a regional private concern with fees charged to either property owners or their financiers, the benefits would be direct given the economic incentives for such a firm to ensure that code compliance was undertaken. Such entities could also enter into cost sharing arrangements with banks and insurance companies as well as property owners, to share the costs more broadly.

For structural measures, information exists on demonstrably worthwhile mitigation technologies. However, a major exception relates to catastrophe event return period probabilities which are essential in determining the cost/benefit trade offs of different types of mitigation actions. For this, historical patterns are limited to a few centuries; also changing and/or unmeasured patterns (e.g., Greenhouse effect and El Niño) exacerbate the challenges of forecasting frequency probabilities.

However, even the extensive information available is too seldom articulated in layman language of practical use by those who should derive the most implementation benefits. These include development decision-makers as well as professionals and artisans in the construction (and retrofitting) fields. Recommended reading includes: *Managing Natural Hazards to Reduce Loss (OAS, Disasters, Planning and Development: Managing Natural Hazards to Reduce Loss, 1990).*

Strategies Linked to Insurance Usage

For non-structural technologies, clear and durable on-the-ground markers could disseminate valuable information. Such could display floodwater and wave surge expected levels. Structural information techniques could include sample skeleton structures (perhaps mobile) which would display practical retrofitting installations. More than anything however, is the need for government, civic and private, (including insurance companies) to grasp initiatives for mitigation implementation.

There is no empirical data on self-insurance usage. Public utilities (CARILEC and Barbados L&P) have such programs which include stand-by credit mechanisms to provide liquidity during build-up of the self-insurance funding amounts. An argument can be made for tax deductibility of such dedicated funding, as the considerations are analogous to the tax deductibility allowed insurance companies for essentially the same purposes.

So-called 'Captive' insurance company arrangements contain self-insurance features. Here industry affinity groups, e.g., Caribbean Hotels Association, enter into insurance purchasing combinations. These can include the joint capitalization of an offshore captive insurance company, which could have the function of carrying the 'claims deductible' exposure of shareholder property owners in the manner described earlier. This is an example of risk and reinsurance pooling.

In the wider socioeconomic context, the broad-brush practices used for risk rating, serve to discourage building structure vulnerability reduction measures. Outside the Caribbean such measures are very prevalent and of proven effectiveness to mitigate catastrophe destruction and disruption. Insurance companies, with full concurrence of their reinsurers, offer significant premium rate differentials conditioned on the specific location and physical risk characteristics of properties insured.

Empirical data showing the vulnerability reduction (VR) cost/benefit yield potential is not standardized. However, a respected ESC civil engineering firm (CEP Engineering Ltd.) compiled the following table to summarize estimates of the VR measure expenditures required to reduce by 50% the Probable Maximum Loss (PML) from a Category III (120 mph+) hurricane:

Table 3.1: Characteristic Expenditure on VR Measures
Required to Reduce CAT III Hurricane PML by 50 %
Expressed as % of Overall Building Value

	New Construction	*Retrofitting*
Construction Categories:		
Dwellings		
Reinforced concrete and masonry	1.2	1.8
Lightweight roof and masonry walls	1.5	2.2
All lightweight construction	2.2	3.4
Commercial/ Industrial/Public		
Reinforced concrete and masonry	1.3	2.0
Lightweight roof and masonry walls	1.7	2.8
Steel structure and lightweight cladding	2.8	3.8

As an example, a $ 1,000,000 value Class B commercial structure, without deliberate VR measures, could typically be assessed at a 10% ($100,000) PML for a Category III hurricane.

Estimates suggest that VR measures costing $17,000 (new) or $28,000 (retrofitted) would reduce the PML by 50% to $50,000.

Hurricane Vulnerability Reduction (VR) Measures for Structures

Cost/Benefit Yield Estimates. The methodology for determining VR cost estimates to yield a 50% reduction in Probable Maximum Loss (PML) from a Category III hurricane (Saffir-Simpson scale, above 120 mph wind speed) is illustrated below. This category storm is generally recognized by insurance markets for damage exposure estimations.

The approach used[12] was first, to express the Category III maximum wind speed as one minute pounds per square foot pressure. As the mean value, the figure of 2.25% was employed, representing the estimate of the incremental VR measures' cost for a new dwelling structure. This figure was deduced from 20 years' of professional experience on both design and retrofitting consulting as well as many on-the-spot surveys of post-hurricane damage scenarios. Original estimates were compared and adjusted using other information sources including Munich Re's published (worldwide) materials. In particular findings showed:

---

[12] Source: Gibbs, A., CEP

1.   Not unexpectedly VR retrofitting proves more expensive than VR measures implemented at the time of original construction.

2.   Caribbean *industrial* purpose structures, as opposed to regular commercial structures, customarily have the least storm resistive designs and materials.

3.   From insurers' observations, storm damage to contents characteristically runs twice the damage cost to the respective structures.

Following that, the 2.25% mean was scaled to VR cost estimates for the several construction and occupancy use classes. The methodology and judgement incorporates reasonable confidence on the potential of VR measures, at the indicated cost levels, being able to reduce hurricane damage (and PMLs) by 50%. This confidence is founded on post-hurricane surveying and information from clients who have adopted similar VR measure recommendations.

It should be made clear that estimates shown in the table are necessarily broad averages for the classes shown. Individual structures have individual structural, exposure, and location characteristics which can vary their VR performance from the averages displayed.

Table 3.2: Illustration of Impact of Hurricane Vulnerability Reduction (VR) Measures on the Risk Premium/Risk Amount Ratio

	Risk Premium/Risk Amount Ratios	
	Before VR Measures	*After VR Measures*
	$	$
Sum Insured	500,000	500,000
PML %	10%	5%
PML $	50,000	25,000
Claim Deductible 2 %	10,000	10,000
Net Insurance Liability	40,000	15,000
CAT premium rate %	0.60%	0.45%
CAT Premium $	3,000	2,250
Ratios:		
a. Risk Premium/Risk Amount	**7.50%** (3,000/40,000)	**15.0%** (2,250/15,000)
b. 1/a	**13.3**	**6.7**

Notes/Assumptions:

Building Structure Hurricane PML:

Before VR retrofitting	10%
After VR retrofitting	5%

Policy Claim deductible is 2% times sum insured

Sum Insured is $500,000

Premium rates (%) are: (CAT) Element	Full rate	Catastrophe
Without VR measures	1.00	0.60
With VR measures	0.75	0.45

Source: Gibbs, A., CEP

The illustration shows that implementation of VR measures, after a CAT premium rate reduction of 25 % (0.60 to 0.45), has served to decrease the Risk / Premium ratio ('b') from 13.3 to 6.7 -- an improvement of almost 50%.

Clearly, the above measures, if disseminated and implemented across the capital stock assets of Caribbean countries, would not only dramatically reduce post disaster economic strain on the government and on private individuals, but would also permit much broader usage of the insurance mechanism as a less costly policy and risk management tool. While the analysis of pooling and risk transfer in the subsequent chapters is based on existing premiums based on current but limited VR practices, the incorporation of such VR practices on a broad scale could potentially halve the price of insurance protection and thus broaden its usage on a much wider scale. One sector, however, which requires special attention and which to-date is not equipped to afford insurance or be insurable, are the low income communities which remain the responsibility of regional governments in terms of disaster assistance and recovery.

Developing Insurance for Low Income Communities

One of the primary challenges for governments in disaster prone regions, is the protection of low income communities and the development of incentives for community participation in risk management measures. The properties, particularly the housing stock of low income communities is generally fragile, and this fact makes them difficult to insure even if affordability was not an issue. However, affordability is also an issue, therefore, governments have the dual challenge of (i) promoting structural measures to reduce the vulnerability of low income housing assets and (ii) improve economic welfare of such communities to begin allowing a phased in process of risk management using the insurance mechanism.

Due to the above factors, it is imperative that governments in disaster prone countries such as the Caribbean, exploit to the fullest extent the range of tools available for hazard mitigation in order to reduce exposures of low income dwellings, while at the same time making transparent what the government risk liability consists of and what risk liabilities should be borne by the communities themselves. This sort of strategy calls for a two-track approach whereby public funds for 'mitigation works' are made available to these communities in exchange for an explicit public insurance policy which is limited in its coverage but which allows low income communities to be adequately protected if they follow the appropriate practices of vulnerability reduction. Non-participating individuals or communities, while not completely exempt from aid in the event of a major catastrophe, would nevertheless receive second priority than those homeowners who had taken pro-active measures at mitigation and who thus would be explicitly covered for insurance purposes and up to a specified limit, by the government. Such a system would engender inter-community competition in vulnerability reduction measures and at the same time raise the level of awareness regarding the nature of insurance policies and risk sharing.

It should be noted that the implementation of a public insurance scheme such as the one outlined below, is a medium to long term endeavor which requires a process of not only self management of risks, but also an educational process to ensure that affected communities are well versed in the risk framework (both physical and regulatory) in which they operate. Initial financing for the required mitigation measures under such a scheme can be provided via public and international donor funds, as well as through potential savings generated through insurance pooling mechanisms using alternative risk transfer instruments as described in chapter V. In the latter case, an explicit 'social compact' with the insurance industry would be required for such contributions to be viable, although such a compact would also help to promote the practice and understanding of insurance in low income communities for eventual usage; income levels and structural standards permitting.

Below is diagrammed one potential financial structure for a public insurance fund which would combine the aspects of mitigation with education and promotion of insurance.

**Figure 3.1: Outline of a Public Insurance Scheme for the Protection
of Low Income Communities**

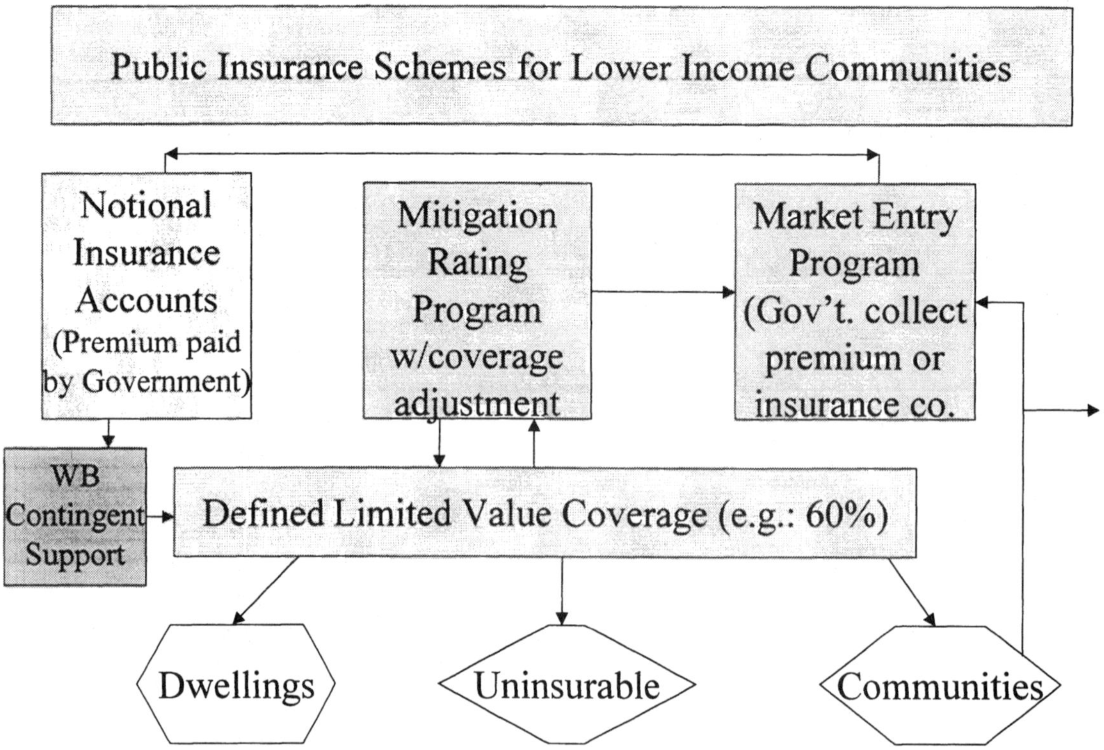

```
┌─────────────────────────────────────────────────────────────────┐
│  Public Insurance Schemes for Lower Income Communities            │
└─────────────────────────────────────────────────────────────────┘

┌──────────────┐     ┌──────────────┐     ┌──────────────────┐
│  Notional    │     │  Mitigation  │     │  Market Entry    │
│  Insurance   │     │  Rating      │     │  Program         │
│  Accounts    │     │  Program     │     │  (Gov't. collect │
│ (Premium paid│     │  w/coverage  │     │  premium or      │
│by Government)│     │  adjustment  │     │  insurance co.   │
└──────────────┘     └──────────────┘     └──────────────────┘

┌──────────┐    ┌──────────────────────────────────────────────┐
│   WB     │    │  Defined Limited Value Coverage (e.g.: 60%)  │
│Contingent│ →  │                                              │
│ Support  │    └──────────────────────────────────────────────┘
└──────────┘

      ⬡ Dwellings      ◇ Uninsurable      ⬡ Communities
```

Source: World Bank

The above scheme relies on a three phase approach which begins with the essential element of mitigation and incentives for vulnerability reduction. As mentioned earlier, the financing for such a phase will likely require public contributions in terms of funding for materials and in some cases skilled technicians. However, the labor cost, for the purposes of risk sharing, would be borne by the communities themselves, as this would be necessary to assure buy-in of the program with the subsequent incentives for obtaining explicit government insurance protection.

The government insurance program would attempt to explicitly define the levels of loss covered by the public sector in the event of a major catastrophe. In this regard, it can be compared to central banking/deposit insurance policy in the financial sector whereby moral hazard is reduced by having the government provide some insurance (in that case to depositors) while limiting the upside loss amounts. In the case of catastrophe insurance, the same principle would apply, i.e., following the verification of structural mitigation measures undertaken by such communities (which would reduce asset risk exposure), the government would provide explicit coverage in an amount that for example, could reach 40%-60% of the property value if this was lost on account of a natural disaster. To support the seriousness of the policy, the government would issue insurance policies to all such homeowners or dwellers showing the level of coverage and the notional actuarially fair premium to be fully subsidized by the government at the outset.

The initial notional premium would therefore constitute no charge to the policy holder, however, the government would make it explicit from an accounting standpoint in order to disseminate the nature and cost of such an insurance policy. The government would also specify in the policy statement what the structural rating grade of the property was since that would provide an input into the notional premium price paid by the government. Of course the government would not be actually paying a premium unless it deemed it prudent to build up reserves for such an event (an option which could be viable in some jurisdictions), but it would hold the liability to pay for damages in the event of a disaster.

The rating category shown on the policy holder's statement would also be reviewed periodically based on progress in the mitigation programs undertaken, and adjusted accordingly. For those properties undertaking significant mitigation measures, the government could safely increase the coverage for the same notional premium (or reduce the premium for the same coverage), an adjustment which would be budget neutral from its standpoint, but which would provide incentive signals to low income dwellers to continue undertaking vulnerability reduction measures if they wish to partake of increased government insurance protection. Eventually, as income levels increased in such communities or parts thereof, the government could begin phasing in cost recoveries on its notional premiums so that property owners themselves began paying for some of their insurance. At such a stage, property owners would also have the option to use insurance from the private markets if deemed to be on more favorable terms.

A key question which might be raised about such a scheme relates to the possible moral hazards, that is, if a given property holder decided to do nothing at all, wouldn't he/she naturally count on government aid anyway, in the event of a natural disaster? The response to this is yes, but a very qualified yes. In other words, the government would not be able to completely ignore a low income property dweller following a disaster, simply because he/she had not signed up for the mitigation program and the public insurance policy. However, the government could prioritize post-disaster reconstruction and give preference to those communities who had undertaken pro-active measures and whose 'insurance policies' would therefore be honored in a timely manner. This measure in itself, if made explicit by the government could encourage inter-community competition to sign up for the mitigation/insurance program in order to receive funding first following a disaster.

While this system does not solve all of the issues of free riders and moral hazards, it does initiate a process of education about risk management and insurance, which in the long run could provide its own societal incentives for communities to reduce their passive reliance on government help, particularly if such help and its timeliness will be prioritized according to risk sharing measures undertaken a priori by other communities.

Mitigation and Insurance as Simultaneous and Sequential Strategies

This chapter has discussed the powerful tool of mitigation as a core strategy in a comprehensive risk management program. It has shown how mitigation measures and insurance policies go hand in hand as two sides of the same coin in the process of risk management. Nevertheless, once all mitigation measures have been exhausted, countries exposed to natural disasters still require mechanisms to "hedge" the remaining risks which constitute economic or financial risks which would be difficult to avoid even by undertaking the most comprehensive vulnerability reduction measures. Such hedging mechanisms which are embodied in the established insurance practice can be structured in different configurations for the purpose of managing and transferring risk. The following chapter describes how the insurance sector in the Caribbean has structured its insurance arrangements with the international market for this purpose. It examines the implications of these arrangements in terms of managing the financial impacts of potential natural catastrophes, including the coverage benefits and premium costs of various strategies.

IV. FINANCIAL STRUCTURE OF REINSURANCE CONTRACTS IN THE ESC

The transfer of risk for potential catastrophic liabilities constitutes a key financial strategy in the economic management of disaster prone countries. Risk transfer in the insurance sector generally takes the form of reinsurance contracts taken by local insurers with international (re)insurers who can better absorb large risks. This chapter examines the current practice and structure of reinsurance arrangements used in the Caribbean and the alternative approaches used for structuring reinsurance contracts. In particular the modalities of proportional reinsurance treaties versus excess-of-loss treaties or their combination are explored to show the advantages and limitations of each. Such financial arrangements set the basis for examining the range of alternative risk transfer instruments which can be deployed under pooled catastrophe funds to manage large loss risks effectively. The structure of these contracts point to the development of future strategies which can deploy a more optimal balance between capital for domestic risk retention and capital for financing the cost of risk transfer.

IV. FINANCIAL STRUCTURE OF REINSURANCE CONTRACTS IN THE ESC

This section starts by setting out the components of *'proportional'* or *'quota share'* reinsurance arrangements. These have by far the most prevalent use by Caribbean insurance companies for their catastrophe reinsurance purposes. Also displayed is a simplified income statement using the described components. There follows a discussion of Excess of Loss (XL) reinsurance with an explanation of why this mechanism, in wide use elsewhere, is not favored in the Caribbean. The section continues with a discussion of some fundamentals of reinsurance portfolio risk management in the context of Caribbean catastrophe insurance.

Table 4.1: Sample Caribbean Insurance Company's Property Insurance Portfolio and Reinsurance Arrangements

Assumptions:

$ Million

1. Insurer's total property (Fire etc. and Catastrophe perils) policy sums insured, i.e., total gross exposure liabilities. 100.00

2. Hurricane peril Estimated Expected Loss (EPL) assessed at average 20% x sums insured = Gross EPL 20.00

3. Average policy claims deductible is 2% times sums insured 2.00

4. Net of deductible aggregate portfolio catastrophe Gross EPL 18.00

5. Average all peril policy premium rate is 0.8% times sums insured – Producing portfolio premiums (Original Gross Premium-OGP) 0.80

6. Gross premium rate (# 5) is comprised of:

Non-catastrophe element (Fire perils, etc.)	0.32%
Catastrophe peril element	0.48%
Total	0.80%

7. Company's direct (before reinsurance) administrative and acquisition expense ratio for property insurance is 30% times OGP (# 5).

8. Reinsurers allow reinsurance commission rates of:

On non-catastrophe premiums ceded	32.5 %
On catastrophe premiums ceded	25.0 %
Average reinsurance commission rate	28.0 %

9. Proportional Reinsurance (i.e. not Excess of Loss) across whole portfolio is structured as 80% reinsured and 20% retained.

10. Respective Catastrophe Liabilities of primary insurer and reinsurers are therefore allocated as:

	Primary Insurer	Reinsurers	Total
$ million			
Gross Sums Insured	20.00	80.00	100.00
Catastrophe aggregate EPL (net of deductibles)	3.60	14.40	18.00

11. Gross Claims are:

        $

Non-Catastrophe		$ 250,000
Catastrophe – Gross	$ 500,000	
Less deductibles $ 100,000 =		$ 400,000
		$ 650,000

12. Investment Income is assumed at 10% of net premium + reinsurance commissions + carry over liquid investment balances   = $44,000

Table 4.2. Simplified Income Statement for Primary (Reinsured) Insurance Company's Property Portfolio

Assumption	Entries	Income	Expense	Net Balance
1	Gross Premiums Received	800,000		
7	Direct Expenses		240,000	
9	80% Reinsurance Premium		640,000	
8	28% Reins. Commission	179,200		
12	Investment Income	44,000		143,200
11	Incurred Eligible Claims		650,000	
9	Claims recoveries from reinsurers (80%)	520,000		13,200

The above example displays the fundamental financial parameters in most common use in the Caribbean for risk pooling utilizing the *proportional (quota share)* reinsurance mechanism.

XL (Excess of Loss) Reinsurance employed in Conjunction with Proportional Reinsurance

Caribbean insurers with proportional reinsurance contracts customarily purchase an 'inner' layer of XL reinsurance to protect their catastrophe peril only net retention. This XL reinsurance covers approximately the upper 20% layer of the retained (co-insured) risk under the main proportional reinsurance contract. Reinsurance costs for proportional covers are essentially a function of the gross premium rates and the reinsurance commission rates allowed as related to the direct administrative costs (assumption # 7 in the example) of the insurance company. For the sake of simplicity, the inner XL catastrophe reinsurance cover is not shown in the above income statement example.

An insurance company, to select the threshold point for an inner XL cover, will primarily consider its net worth strength as well as the additional cost of the XL cover. As an example using the sample shown above, the company had (net of reinsurance) property insurance premiums of $160,000 (20% of gross), which could suggest the company having notional capital for allocation to property business of some $40,000 (a 4:1 premium/capital ratio). The company's remaining capital and any free reserves (retained profits, etc.) could also be considered. Conceivably this company could have selected a $120,000 threshold, above which, it would utilize an XL catastrophe reinsurance cover which would thus allow ceding 25% of the retained risk.

In the above example, a $120,000 threshold retention would have allowed invoking $10,000 in excess of loss cover (gross claims of $650,000 times 20% = $130,000 retained claims, or $10,000 above the XL reinsurance attachment point).

XL Reinsurance Employed as a Principal Mechanism for Catastrophe Reinsurance

The *Excess of Loss* (XL) reinsurance mechanism is widely used outside the Caribbean (by relatively larger insurers) for their catastrophe reinsurance needs. Under XL structures the reinsurers' liabilities are triggered above a given retention amount and customarily for 100% of aggregated claims above the retention amount. The XL reinsurance price is normally expressed as a 'rate on line' signifying the dollar reinsurance premium as a percentage of reinsured loss limit. This rate on line is assessed by judging the extent to which a reinsured portfolio's aggregate EPL would penetrate the reinsured layer's limits. For example, a reinsurance rate on line of 30% ($300,000 per million of limit) would suggest a fully penetrated (exposed) layer and an approximate 3-year notional payback period; i.e., a high frequency and severity probability to reinsurers. As the reinsured limit layers get higher and further removed from anticipated full exposure penetration, the rates on line diminish and the pay back periods increase. Reinsurance commission is not a feature of XL covers.

The accurate and reasonable pricing of XL reinsurance calls for meticulous assessment of a primary portfolio's aggregate catastrophe EPL liabilities. Short of having full information a reinsurer will price to cover the 'doubt' factor and resulting quotations will often deter prospective primary company customers. Primary companies can on occasion be dazzled by the front end cash flow benefits of XL reinsurance without prudently assessing the potential back end liabilities represented by having full liability for the retention limit – a liability actualized by a catastrophe event. XL reinsurance is generally considered as more of a 'bet' than proportional reinsurance under which the respective claims liabilities between reinsured and reinsurer are clearly apportioned from the lowest claims level to the highest. Thinly capitalized primary companies as seen in the Caribbean are understandably averse to full XL reinsurance.

Second Event Reinsurance (Reinstatement Contracts). This is primarily a feature of XL reinsurance contracts and refers to the basic premise that the reinsured limits are available once during a single contract period (normally annual). Once reinsured limits are 'consumed' by a catastrophe event or other claims, the limits require reinstating for 'second (or subsequent) event' via payment of additional reinsurance premium. Most primary companies in the ESC purchase second event coverage reinstatement as included in their original XL contract negotiations as this is generally both cheaper and more likely to be available than having to face reinsurers' quotations in the aftermath of a major claims event. Customarily, 'second event' protection is not an issue under proportional reinsurance contracts where reinsurers contract to reinsure a portfolio's claims for the full contract period.

Reinsurance Portfolio Risk Management Considerations

This report has discussed the proportional catastrophe reinsurance mechanism from the standpoint of the primary insurer. From the standpoint of the reinsurer, the parameters are essentially the converse with the reinsurer entering reinsurance premiums net of commissions, any claims incurred, and any income derivable from invested funds – primarily unexpired premium reserves or reserves for reported, but yet to be paid, claims. However, having a portfolio of reinsurance contracts allows the reinsurer to adopt risk management practices analogous to those practiced by banks on loan portfolios. To obtain an optimum match between risk and return, the reinsurer can reinsure further ('retrocede') to other reinsurers (perhaps with reciprocity), as well as consider securitization to contain liability. However, throughout the chain of risk bearing (from policy issuing insurer, to reinsurer, to retrocession carrier, to securitization), the key parameter is the relationship, or the ratio of Risk Premium to Risk Amount.

In the context of catastrophe insurance, the value of 'Risk Amount' is comprised of:

- Severity element – the Probable Maximum Loss (PML) and

- Frequency element – the probability of a catastrophe event.

For the severity element, proven technologies exist to obtain reasonably accurate quantification. These require detailed hazard mapping and awareness of distinctive building structure methods and materials. The frequency element assessment has yet to attain a similar stature of reliable precision. Actuarial approaches to catastrophe event return periods can be reasonably viewed as volatile for reinsurers' short term practical purposes. Furthermore, the 'Greenhouse' and El Niño theories suggest that historic natural disaster frequency patterns are unlikely to be repeated. Thus the forecasting of catastrophe frequencies has yet to mature to a reliable level in calculable risk probability terms.

These factors –severity and frequency - are those which underpin the catastrophe reinsurance markets' cycles. In effect, Risk Premium levels prove almost invariably either too high or too low, and only fortuitously are rarely in equilibrium to the Risk Amount exposure.

In the Caribbean, the existing severity (PML) assessment techniques are very broad brush. Characteristically, a portfolio's aggregate PML is established by reinsurers' view of hurricane storm tracks and impact potentials. Wide geographic areas containing several nations are customarily swept into a single PML category without regard for the topographical features and structure resistance distinctions propounded by regional and international experts.

Furthermore, Caribbean insurers' catastrophe premium rates are also very broad brush without discrimination to reflect topographical hazard and structure resistance distinctions. It can therefore be logically held that the poorer risk quality properties are subsidized in premium rate terms by the better risk quality properties. These broad brush reinsurance and policy rating practices may have produced administrative simplicity but cannot claim effectiveness as regards accuracy in assessing the Risk Premium : Risk Amount ratio.

Capital market alternatives, whether they be in the form of securities such as bonds or in the form of loans, can potentially reduce or at least stabilize the prices of coverage. The reasons are twofold: the capital markets comprise approximately $42 trillion in assets currently compared with insurance industry capital estimated at $0.9 trillion, and second, investors have shown portfolio preferences in purchasing catastrophe bonds given that their yields are both higher than the market and uncorrelated with global financial market movement, thus providing a diversifying hedge. Although such bonds have 'default' characteristics in the sense that if a disaster strikes, the bonds are liable to lose interest and principal, the probability of such events is generally lower than similarly rated sovereign bonds which have higher probabilities of country default risk.

Before considering in the next chapter, the cost effectiveness in the pricing of alternative risk transfer instruments such as catastrophe bonds or contingent credit lines, Figure 4.1 illustrates the catastrophe insurance coverages and their structures:

Figure 4.1: Combined Proportional (Quota Share) Treaty with Catastrophe Excess of Loss (XL) Reinsurance Structure

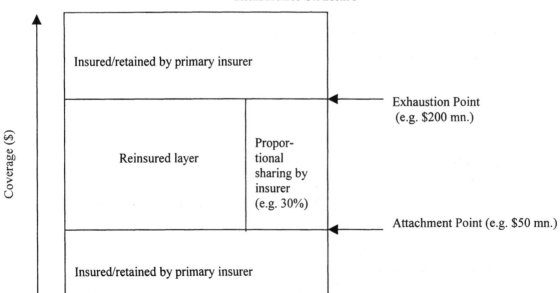

Source: Goldman Sachs

The above example shows a reinsurance structure which combines the elements of proportional treaty coverage (used widely in the ESC) and excess of loss (XL) covers. As mentioned above, local insurance companies in the ESC traditionally use proportional treaties (also known as quota share treaties) to share risks with reinsurers. The above diagram implies that after the initial retention of risk by the primary local insurer at the lower levels, the primary insurer then cedes about 70% of the coverage (and premiums) to the international reinsurer. For any claim based on damage, the insurer would thus pay 30% and the reinsurer 70% (past the initial retention level and before the exhaustion point).

Generally in the East Caribbean, the proportional treaties do not have upper limits as in the above diagram, although more recently proportional reinsurers have begun limiting their upper layer liability. As discussed above, local companies in the ESC, have begun utilizing excess of loss (XL) cover on what they retain, i.e., on the 30% portion in this case. As a matter of practice, however, XL cover as a form of insurance/reinsurance is not based on proportion of total claims submitted but rather on a specified level of quantified losses (independent of the claim amount). The XL reinsurance cover begins paying after the 'attachment point' and stops paying if losses exceed the 'exhaustion point' or cumulative limit.

The above structure combines both methods in that claims are paid by the reinsurer based on attachment and exhaustion limits, though within those limits, the primary reinsurer also shares a small proportion of the risks, or what is also known as 'coinsurance'. These structures provide strong incentives for all parties to be concerned about loss reduction measures and to avoid adverse selection problems. However, as is discussed later, the ESC catastrophe reinsurance structure is different from the above model in that an even greater proportion of risk is ceded or transferred (see diagram below). While this makes sense from a macroeconomic perspective, it can lead to disincentives for loss reduction measures if very little risk is retained/managed, and because of the high dependence on reinsurance, it leads to more potential volatility in the pricing of catastrophe insurance which is subject to the global market supply availability.

Figure 4.2: Typical Caribbean Reinsurance Treaty Structure

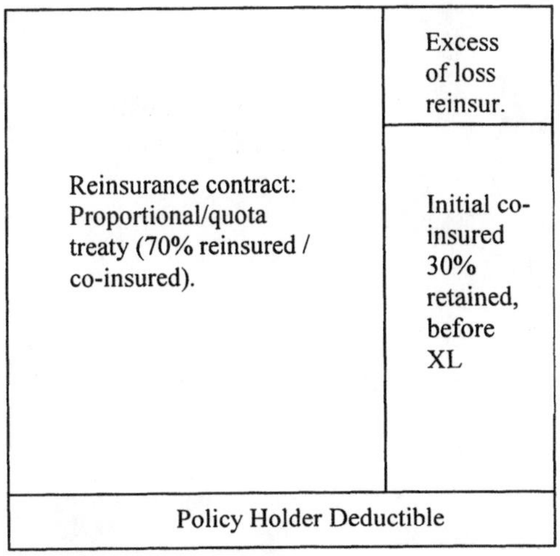

	Excess of loss reinsur.
Reinsurance contract: Proportional/quota treaty (70% reinsured / co-insured).	Initial co-insured 30% retained, before XL
Policy Holder Deductible	

Source: World Bank

The determination of whether pooled structures coupled with alternative risk transfer instruments can be more cost effective, requires an analysis of the current structure of reinsurance arrangements in the East Caribbean market. As mentioned above, the primary reinsurance medium consists of the quota or proportional treaty which absorbs the larger portion of the risks written in the region. In order to evaluate the suitability of instruments (either risk financing or risk transfer) which utilize excess of loss type covers (XL), the pricing of the existing quota treaties needs to be compared on equivalent terms with XL rates.

Quota treaties are priced based on primary insurance rates, i.e., the premium over the sum insured is charged to the primary insurer minus the commission received by that primary insurer from the reinsurer. Conceptually, however, the 'layers' of loss coverage implicit in a quota treaty arrangement should be similarly priced to those under XL arrangements after taking into account differential transaction costs.

Table 4.3 illustrates this approach for the East Caribbean, i.e., using rate averages currently in effect in the OECS, Barbados and Trinidad and Tobago: At the left side of the table, a proportional/quota treaty based on a EPL of 10% and a weighted average premium of 0.59% of sums insured is illustrated. Applying the premium cost over the product of EPL and value insured, this yields a rate-on-line (ROL) premium equivalent of approximately 5.9% before taking into account commissions paid. After subtracting commissions to cover business acquisition and administrative costs (28% of premium ceded), the result is a net 4.2% ROL equivalent.

The 10% EPL is used based on the more diversified reinsurer's portfolio which further minimizes portfolio risk to below the individual company average EPLs in the region (15%-20%). As can be observed, the gross ROL figure derived from the quota treaty is equivalent to the average of all ROL layers shown at the middle and left of the table. Here, each level of loss is shown along with its respective probability of occurrence and ROL premium. At the rightmost side, the weighted sum of the various ROLs yields an average ROL of 5.9% as well.

Table 4.3: Analysis of ROL Rates and Proportional Treaty Equivalents - East Caribbean

Insured Val. Treaty a/	EPL	Prem.	Coverage Point	Coverage Layer	Prob.	ROL	Spread	Weighted ROL Rate
$ 100.00	10%	0.6%	5.7%	5.7%	15.00%	17.00%	2.0%	1.0%
			10.0%	4.3%	11.00%	14.00%	3.0%	0.6%
ROL Eqv.	5.9%		14.3%	4.3%	7.50%	10.79%	3.3%	0.5%
			21.4%	7.1%	5.30%	8.30%	3.0%	0.6%
less rein.			28.6%	7.1%	3.50%	6.64%	3.1%	0.5%
commis.	4.2%		35.7%	7.1%	2.50%	5.80%	3.3%	0.4%
			42.9%	7.1%	1.50%	4.90%	3.4%	0.4%
			50.0%	7.1%	1.20%	4.20%	3.0%	0.3%
			57.1%	7.1%	0.75%	3.90%	3.2%	0.3%
			64.3%	7.1%	0.70%	3.80%	3.1%	0.3%
			71.4%	7.1%	0.35%	3.50%	3.2%	0.3%
			85.7%	14.3%	0.18%	3.40%	3.2%	0.5%
			100.0%	14.3%	0.15%	3.35%	3.2%	0.5%
				100.0%				5.9%

a. Assumes after deductible under proportional/quota share reinsurance treaty.
Source: World Bank

A summary of the above ROL pricing structure at selected probability levels is illustrated below:

Figure 4.3: Current Reinsurance Rates at Disaster Probability Points

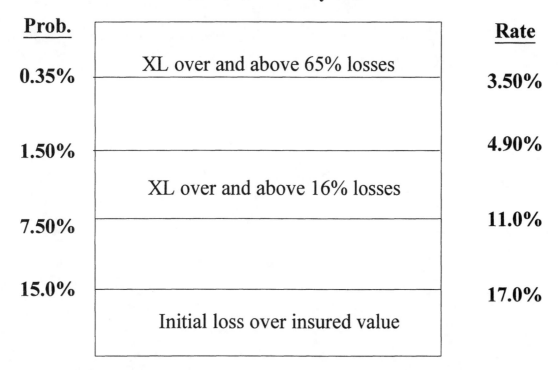

Source: World Bank

Figure 4.3, thus, serves to show that reinsurance rates-on-line are consistent with primary premium rates under proportional/quota treaties. Nevertheless, it also shows that well managed low-cost local companies stand to gain from reinsurance commissions received when these more than cover their expenses. However, it also means that local ESC companies may have biases towards higher premiums as these in turn receive higher reinsurance commissions, all else being equal.

The above (second illustration), however, also shows that reinsurance arrangements at various levels of risk can be tailor-made to improve the coverage/cost ratio of insurers and policyholders depending on the level of risk transferred abroad and the amount retained as "own" capital. Since premium rates decline at the higher (less probable) layers of loss, this provides a number of financial structuring opportunities to optimize pricing, assuming a larger retention of risk at the lower levels where reinsurance is most costly.

Recently the capital markets (both bond and credit markets) have entered the reinsurance business through the provision of alternative risk transfer and financing instruments which are geared towards providing special purpose excess of loss covers, particularly at the highest loss levels. These developments are examined further in the next chapter to demonstrate how, under certain risk sharing arrangements, such instruments can provide efficiently priced sources of capital to fund insured risks. In addition, they can allow domestic insurers who pool their capital and increase risk reserves, to leverage retained capital in ways that can help to increase local insurance capacity. This would permit a reduction in the sensitivity of local insurance coverage to external supply crunches.

V. TRANSFERRING CATASTROPHIC RISKS TO THE CAPITAL MARKET

A number of events have prompted capital market institutions to enter the catastrophe reinsurance business during the last decade. In particular, some of the colossal disasters experienced in the 1990s demonstrated the vulnerability of even the largest global insurers, and the observation that reasonable "reference" scale disasters which could be expected, still have the potential to disrupt the insurance markets if events occur at frequencies slightly above the norm. It was almost inevitable given the sheer size of the capital markets, that capital from such sources would eventually be channeled to fund insurance risks directly. However, since capital market institutions are not typically risk underwriters in the classic insurance sense, the instruments developed to fund or 'securitize' risk sometimes have particular properties for measuring risk which are tailored towards the investor community that provides such capital. Capital market participation first manifested itself by way of credit suppliers that provided backing for government/industry partnerships via the financing of the highest layers of potential losses which insurers in disaster prone regions had become reluctant to underwrite. These innovations have appeared primarily in the developed world markets, nevertheless, they can provide immediate opportunities for catastrophe prone countries. In the Caribbean some of these tools can be incorporated as part of their package of policy measures in order to implement sound and sustainable risk management and disaster funding strategies.

V. TRANSFERRING CATASTROPHIC RISKS TO THE CAPITAL MARKET

In response to the capital constraints that might affect global reinsurers (and therefore emerging market insurance sectors) during periods of recurring high frequency catastrophes, and in response to domestic risk aversion by primary insurers in the wake of major disaster events, the need for additional 'risk bearing capacity' and long term funding availability has generated a supply of risk capital from non traditional sources, i.e., the capital and credit markets. While the reinsurance capacity has also increased by way of new industry players such as in the Bermuda market, the catastrophes of the last decade demonstrated that world funding reserves for potentially major events needed to be assured in ways that would not only avoid past cyclical supply/demand capacity constraints and associated price volatility, but also assure the future solvency of major insurance and reinsurance players. The response, therefore of the capital and credit markets, far from being an indication of a replacement of reinsurance, has shown more precisely that both reinsurance and capital market instruments need to work together to best manage large event risks in ways that optimize risk sharing among property owners, primary insurers, reinsurers and capital markets.

The new instruments for managing catastrophe risk are not only used by those wishing to be insured in the traditional sense, but also by major reinsurers themselves who see the advantages of distributing risks to other markets while putting less of their own core capital at risk. Those 'other' markets whose capacities are practically unlimited in terms of financing the potential range of global catastrophic losses, have also the advantage of absorbing financial shocks with little or no 'bounce back' effect through the insurance markets, a characteristic which is particularly beneficial for countries which can be severely affected from the insurance industry cycles following natural disasters. Paradoxically though, the fact that such alternative instruments have entered the world stage, may in-and-of-themselves, serve to dampen premium volatility which in the past was caused mainly by the absence of alternative capital sources. However, this implies that volatility in pricing may require a permanent presence and utilization of alternative sources of risk capital by insurance industries throughout the world. This would be to maintain the supply of such capital available while global insurance capital grows incrementally until it reaches a new plateau where catastrophic events might be more fully insured and funded. Both governments as well as private sector players in emerging economies can partake of such tools by pooling sufficient capital to allow accessing these alternative forms of risk financing and risk transfer.

Risk Financing Arrangements

One of the initial forms in which the capital markets got involved in paying for catastrophic losses was through financing arrangements for pooled structures. This took the form of a line of credit that was syndicated to banks, insurance companies and other lenders. The primary benefit of such an arrangement was that it made large sums of funds immediately available and was meant as a supplemental source to pay for the potentially very large losses. This was especially helpful in areas where reinsurers had high exposures and additional capacity was an issue. Another benefit of a credit facility was its relative cost in terms of having funds available to pay for losses. The commitment fee ranged from 0.25% to 0.375% per annum and the borrowing cost had a range between 0.75% to 1.5% over LIBOR for a term of up to 7 years. The disadvantage with a financing arrangement is that any amounts availed of, would have to be repaid together with interest.

In order to enter into a financing arrangement, a distinct source of repayment had to be established and pledged to the lender(s) as security. This distinct source of repayment took the form of an assessment or surcharge to policyholders of a pool or, more often, spread to a broader base, typically all policyholders in a state. The California Earthquake Authority had the former, while the Hawaii Hurricane Relief Fund and the Florida funds adopted the latter approach (see last section of this chapter). The order in which the credit facility was utilized in relation to the other claims paying sources (cash on hand, reinsurance, member company assessments, etc.) was a function of the objectives of the pool. In general, the credit facility was placed at the topmost layer (last to be utilized) since the pools wished to avoid imposing assessments or surcharges to its constituents.

Another form of credit financing that has been employed are pre-event notes. These are bonds that are issued prior to any catastrophic event. The cash proceeds are placed in a trust and can only be utilized to pay for losses. The added advantages of issuing bonds relative to a line of credit are that the bonds have a longer maturity (10 to 30 years), fewer loan covenants, and less pre conditions for the drawing of funds. The disadvantage is that the bonds are generally more expensive than a line of credit facility and require the immediate payment of interest.

The Market for the Securitization of Catastrophe Risk

The securitization of catastrophe risk, that is, the packaging of insurance risks into marketable financial securities, and which is opening new options for catastrophe coverage, is manifested in the private capital markets in the U.S., Europe, and Japan under the following instrumentalities:

Catastrophe Bonds. Catastrophe bonds pay investors high yields, but are subject to default on all or part of principal and interest if a catastrophic event occurs during the life of the bond. Thus investor appeal is based on the high returns with low probabilities of default while the insurer's interest is in obtaining additional reinsurance capacity which is made available for claims payments in the event of a disaster. Funds obtained from bond proceeds are normally invested in risk free instruments which also help the insured to lower the eventual net cost of the interest coupon payments. In order to accommodate the desire of insurers and reinsurers to treat protection attained through catastrophe bonds and derivatives in the same fashion as traditional insurance, the approach in the capital markets has been to create a reinsurance contract between the ceding insurer and a special purpose vehicle (SPV) which then effectively securitizes the contract on the market[13]. Such entities issue catastrophe bonds to investors, and as a

---

[13] In most jurisdictions, without using an SPV, a regulatory drawback of catastrophe bonds is that, unlike straight reinsurance whose premium cost can be deducted from an insurer's gross written premium, the cost of securitizing catastrophe risk cannot be deducted in the same manner. Thus, when considering securitized risk transfer instruments, a risk based capital criteria would appear to favor a company's net surplus position when using straight reinsurance

separate transaction, sell reinsurance to interested insurers who can then take advantage of the more favorable regulatory accounting treatment. The insured party is not subject to any reinsurer 'credit risk' either, as the insurance coverage is fully collateralized.

Contingent Surplus Notes: These financial Notes are essentially 'put' rights which allow the insured party to issue debt to pre-specified buyers in the event of a catastrophic event. The Notes are a risk financing (versus risk transfer) mechanism but under regulatory norms can be considered as part of the insurer's available surplus or capital. The issuance of notes can be done in exchange for cash or liquid assets which are received from investors. Such liquid securities are kept in a trust which, in the event of a disaster, are exchanged via a financial intermediary, for the surplus debt notes issued by the insurer to finance catastrophe loss claims.

Exchange Traded Catastrophe Options. The property claim service (PCS) options which trade on the Chicago Board of Trade as investment instruments, are mechanisms which provide the right of the purchaser to demand payment under an option contract, if the claims index surpasses a pre specified level (the strike price). The indexes used cover different areas of the U.S. (East, MidWest, West) and reflect insurance industry aggregate reported claims which are converted into an industry index. A national index also exists, but the regional indexes permit hedging against large risks in specified areas. The market does not yet constitute a large segment of the insurance market but investors can profit from selling the options in diversified territories which are unlikely to suffer losses simultaneously (with corresponding option pay outs). Use of an index rather than specific claims experience also can result in 'basis risk' , i.e., the risk that specific claims obligations do not necessarily exactly match the compensation amount from the option pay out. A drawback, however, is that insurance companies cannot deduct these costs as premium equivalents.

Catastrophe Equity Puts. Equity puts are also a form of an option which, for a pre-paid fee, permits the insurer to sell equity shares on demand to investors, as a means of funding claims in the wake of a major disaster. Such instruments as in the case of contingent surplus notes, are risk financing instruments and do not actually perform the traditional insurance function of risk transfer, though they provide immediate liquidity.

Catastrophe Swaps. Catastrophe swaps are another method of paying premiums for catastrophe reinsurance. Such swaps use capital market players as counterparties. In a catastrophe swap arrangement, an insurance portfolio with potential payment liabilities are swapped for a security and its associated cash flows. An insurer would take on the obligation to pay an investor periodic payments on a specified security (or portfolio of securities) which the investor was liable for, while conversely, the investor would take on the potential liabilities under an insured portfolio, for example, by making payments for catastrophe losses based on agreed measures of magnitude or severity (e.g.: a catastrophe loss index). For the insurer, payments made on the investor's securities are equivalent to a reinsurance premium.

Weather Derivatives. Weather derivatives are contracts against weather change triggers generally take the form of premium payments for contracts which provide

---

versus having the same coverage using catastrophe bonds. Nevertheless, as discussed, financial markets have devised methods for overcoming such impediments, primarily through the establishment of offshore special purpose reinsurers.

payouts to the "insured" in the event that a pre-defined number of days with a specified time period reach temperatures above or below the trigger point. Farmers in areas subject to crop freeze for example can purchase weather options whereby payment is made if the number of cold days below a certain point go past a pre-defined period and temperature level. Similarly for drought or heat affected areas such weather derivatives can be purchased to invoke payment if hot weather remains in force for a longer forecast period (e.g.: for utility, electric or gas companies). Parties in opposite weather areas can swap positions to insure interested counterparties for such transactions, although speculative investors can also benefit from the premium income earned in the case no trigger is invoked.

One of the earliest examples of successful securitization of catastrophe risks as well as one of the largest amounts of securitized risk done to date, involved the USAA Insurance Company's transaction (7/97 to 6/98) with Residential Re, which was a special purpose reinsurer set up specifically for this purpose. The outline of the structure is shown in figure 5.1.

Figure 5.1: USAA Risk Securitization Transaction

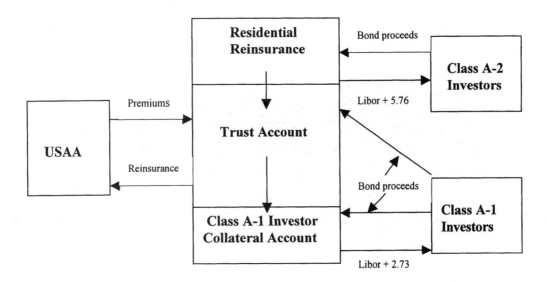

Source: Goldman Sachs

As can be observed, the USAA deal offered cat bonds to Class A-1 and A-2 investors. Class A-1 received a lower bond yield but received protection on the principal in the event of a catastrophe exceeding the 'attachment' point of the contract (i.e.: loss levels reaching up through the reinsurance layer which was covered by the bond). The two flows of bond proceeds shown for the A-1 investors reflect the fact that additional funds beyond reinsurance needs had to be raised in order to place part of the bond proceeds in a Collateral Account where they would be invested to return the principal to those investors. The remainder of the A-1 bond proceeds were kept in the trust account, subject to use in the event of a disaster. The additional interest cost of those extra bond proceeds plus those used for reinsurance funding, was offset by the lower interest rate offered to the class A-1 investors. For the A-2 investors, the yield was much higher as they were subject to losing all principal. Residential Re was the special purpose reinsurer set up to collect the 'premium' payments from USAA and pay for reinsurance 'claims'.

The bonds had a dual trigger which included both hurricane strength and actual loss levels. As a comfort against moral hazard, USAA kept a high retention of risk ($1 bn.) as well as a proportional / quota share reinsurance treaty above that level.

Disaster index contracts or parametric hazard triggers as illustrated below, can also provide an efficient means of setting up insurance contracts since they depend on objectively measurable events to trigger indemnification. This can be useful for the protection of government assets for example, since it skips the 'insurance loss adjustment' stage which requires site-by-site evaluation of damages. One drawback, however, is the 'basis' risk, i.e., the risk that the event 'trigger' does not necessarily correlate with losses on the ground. Nevertheless, this was successfully implemented under Parametric Re, a special purpose reinsurer used by Tokio Marine Insurance to obtain securitized reinsurance against earthquake risk. The 'parametric trigger' was based on earthquake intensity as well as on two grids rings specified around Tokyo and other Japanese cities (an inner and an outer area grid) to determine what reinsurance would be provided in the event of an earthquake.

Table 5.1: Parametric Re: Earthquake Intensity and Grids used as Payout Triggers

Earthquake level: Richter Scale	7.1	7.2	7.3	7.4	7.5	7.6	7.7
% Bond loss: Inner City Grid Epicenter	25%	40%	55%	70%	85%	100%	
% Bond loss: Outer Grid Epicenter			25%	44%	63%	81%	100%

Figure 5.2: Grid Areas for Epicenter Determination

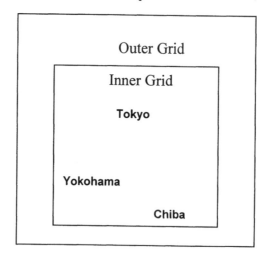

Figure 5.3. Insurance/Reinsurance Flow Structure

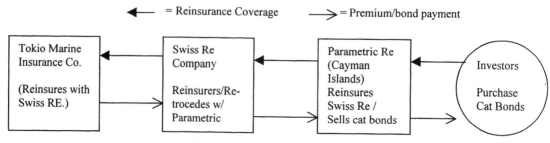

Source: Goldman Sachs 1999.

In line with this type of 'parametric trigger' design, the following illustrates a hypothetical catastrophe bond structure and its issuance terms in which a 'multi-hazard bundle' is incorporated into the risk profile of the bond. While limited bonds of this type have been issued to date, investors wishing to diversify against not only financial market movements, but also against concentrations of single hazards, may find such an issue attractive since some of the hazards (rainfall versus drought) are mutually offsetting.

Structure of a Multi-Peril Catastrophe Bond/Note
Using weather index triggers

Terms of Note: **US $100,000,000 Issue**

    Maturity: 3 years

    Coupon Interest (no event): LIBOR + 4.99

    Expected (probability-adjusted) value of coupon interest: LIBOR + 4.93

    Coupon Interest (post-event): LIBOR - 2.40

    Expected Loss: 0.79% of Face Value (probability adjusted)

    Expected value of yield given principal/coupon interest adjustments: LIBOR + 4.68

    Index triggers for coupon/principal adjustment:

        Earthquake: Richter 7+ quake (specified locations/cities - first event trigger)

        Hurricane: Windspeed 120+ m.p.h.(specified coastal locations - 2nd+ event trigger)

        Flood: Accumulated Rainfall (defined period) 40+ cm.(specified locations - 2nd+ event)

        Drought: Accumulated (defined period) 2- cm. (specified locations - 1st event trigger)

Coupon strip payment	Coupon strip payment	Coupon strip payment	Coupon strip payment
Earthquake Risk	Winsdstorm (hurrica-	Flood (rainfall) risk	Drought (rainfall) risk
LIBOR + 5.5	ne risk) LIBOR+5.0	LIBOR + 4.6	LIBOR + 4.9
(no event)	(no event)	(no event)	(no event)
Post Event Terms:	Post Event Terms:	Post Event Terms:	Post Event Terms:
LIBOR - 3	LIBOR - 2	LIBOR - 2.5	LIBOR -2
Prob.: 0.4%	Prob.: 1.2%	Prob.: 1.1%	Prob.: 0.3%
Weight: 25%	Weight: 25%	Weight: 30%	Weight: 20%

Weighted coupon interest payment above LIBOR (pre-event): 0.25*(5.5)+0.25*(5.0)+0.25*(4.6)+0.20*(4.9)

(no loss of principal) = 4.99 %

		Coupon strip	Weighted weight	rate
Expected value: coupon interest above LIBOR, taking into account event probabilities

			strip	weight	rate
Earthquake risk:	((0.004)*(-3.0)+(1-0.004)*(5.5)) =	5.47	0.25	1.37
Hurricane risk:	((.012)*(-2.0)+(1-0.12)*(5.0)) =	4.92	0.25	1.23
Flood risk:	((.011)*(-2.5)+(1-.011)*(4.6)) =	4.52	0.30	1.36
Drought risk:	((.003)*(-2.0)+(1-.003)*(4.9)) =	4.88	0.20	0.98
			1.00	**4.93**

Weighted coupon interest payment below LIBOR (post-event): 0.25*(-3)+0.25*(-2)+0.3*(-2.5)+0.2*(-2)

(with loss of principal) = -2.40 %

Expected discount on principal, taking into account event probabilities (over 3-yr. period): <u>Loss of Principal</u>

Earthquake risk:	0.004*100*0.25	0.10
Hurricane risk:	0.012*100*0.25	0.30
Flood risk:	0.011*100*0.3	0.33
Drought risk:	0.003*100*0.2	0.06
Total ($US millions)		**0.79**

Expected yield on note/bond taking into account probabilities of loss of interest/principal (post event):

(note: event time is not specified, but averaged out over bond repayment period - assumes annual coupon)

Years:	0	1	2	3	
Cash Flows:	-100	4.93	4.93	4.93	
($US mn.)				99.2	
Total:	-100	4.93	4.93	104.1	Yield (IRR): Libor +4.68%

Source: World Bank

Cost/Benefit Factors in Utilizing Capital Market Instruments

A simple numerical example shows how capital markets can supplement insurance and reduce costs. Assume that a primary insurance company calculates the probability of a loss of more than US$15 million but less than US$25 million at 10 percent. If the primary insurer purchases reinsurance at this rate, it will break even over time. Adding administrative costs, operating costs, and a risk 'load', the reinsurer might charge a premium of 14 percent (10 percent + 4 percent).

Alternatively, the primary insurer could issue a US$10 million bond to investors, then put the US$10 million in U.S. treasury notes paying, say, 5 percent. The investors' principal of US$10 million would be put at risk as part of the contract. If a catastrophe with losses exceeding US$25 million occurs, the investors might lose all their principal. For putting their principal at risk, the investors would demand at least a 17 percent return: 5 percent as risk-free interest, 10 percent for the "pure" risk of losing their principal (akin to a default risk), and 2 percent as an additional risk load. Net of the investment in treasury notes, the insurer's total financing cost would approach 12 percent, compared with the 14 percent for traditional reinsurance at that given level of risk.

Figure 5.4. Institutional/Financial Structure for a Catastrophe Bond Scheme

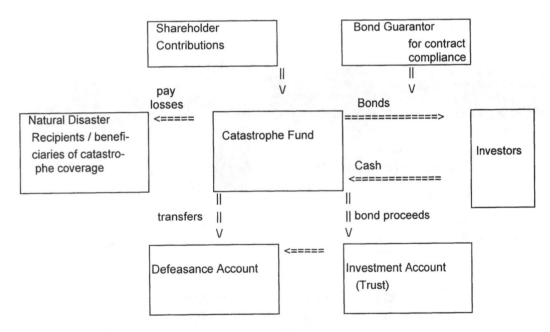

Source: Chase Securities

In the above example, a "Catastrophe Fund" can be privately or publicly owned. In the international private markets as mentioned, this usually takes the form of a "special purpose vehicle" which serves as a legal/financial entity to invest proceeds obtained from catastrophe bonds and pay investors the bond coupon. In the event of an actual catastrophe, funds would be paid to the insured recipients. The defeasance account is used to accumulate funds for repayment of the bond principal if investors are to receive some level of 'principal protection' in the event of a catastrophe event – in this instance, as discussed earlier, the funds raised usually exceed those needed for indemnification since some are set aside solely for the purpose of repaying principal. However, some of these bonds are structured so that the investor loses part or all of the principal and some interest in the event of a catastrophe. The compensation is that the bonds usually pay yields much above the market level for similar 'default risks'.

In yet another option, however, the insurer could arrange a standby credit of US$10 million with a 2 percent commitment charge and an interest rate of 12 percent that kicks in if the loan is needed. If a catastrophe occurs, and assuming a ten-year repayment period for principal (yielding a combined principal plus interest "insurance" cost equivalent to 18 percent), the expected financing cost would be 3.6 percent (0.1 [18 percent] + 0.9 [2 percent]), much lower than with direct reinsurance.

These capital market schemes to supplement insurance have many possible variations. These range from full risk transfer with no financing (where the full principal is at risk, just as in reinsurance) to zero risk transfer with full financing (full repayment of principal). The following diagram illustrates the typical 'full risk transfer' catastrophe bond arrangement showing the pre-event and post-event cash flow payments (post disaster event flows indicated by the dotted lines).

Figure 5.5: Securitizing Catastrophe Risk with Cat Bonds for Creditworthy Disaster Prone Countries

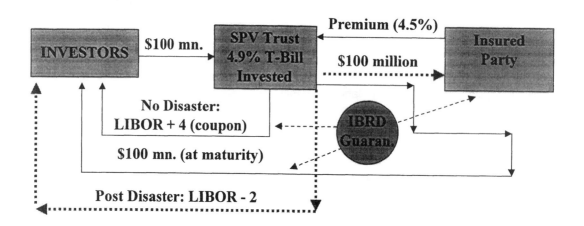

Note: loss event can be defined by objective parameter such as wind speed or earthquake intensity

Source: World Bank, Goldman Sachs, Chase Securities

Implicit in the above structure, is that disaster-prone countries might be sufficiently creditworthy to issue 'cat' bonds for investors to purchase. Support by IBRD in the form of a contractual risk guarantee would enhance the credit rating of such bonds and potentially improve their marketability. The attractiveness of such bond issues could also be enhanced through the use of 'parametric' indicators to trigger eligibility for payment. Such triggers mean that measurable physical events such as wind speed or earthquake intensity at a defined location could trigger the 'insurance payment' instead of using the traditional loss adjustment process based on a structure-by-structure analysis of damage. As discussed in this report, parametric triggers imply some basis risk.

It is difficult to precisely pinpoint why the private sector does not always fully respond to such market needs. The competitive marketplace is a dynamic, ever-changing world where demands and supply are changing constantly in response to underlying societal and natural phenomena. In the case of catastrophe insurance, a new era was formed following Hurricane Andrew which is still in the infant stage of its development. The slowness of the response is partly explained by the extensive legal and regulatory barriers that had grown around the insurance industry over the past century, and which required some modifications. For example, in the case of Cat Bonds, even in developed economies, substantial time was spent obtaining opinions and rulings from various jurisdictions stating that investors purchasing such bonds would neither be acting as unlicensed insurers or violating anti-gambling laws. Substantial additional time elapsed working with insurance regulators to assure that such bonds purchased by insurers would be assessed their risk based capital on bonds, and not as higher risk securities which carry a more punitive rate. Other regulatory issues pertained to disclosure, listing and timing requirements, withholding taxes, and revisiting the definition of insurance; aspects where the multilateral development institutions can be crucial in accelerating market development.

A factor which could greatly assist the development of an ESC reinsurance pool would be the recent legislation in some Caribbean countries, e.g., Trinidad and Tobago, and Barbados allowing for a tax deductible catastrophe reserve. An ESC reinsurance pool would benefit from this provision.

Catastrophe Programs Around the World

Japan, New Zealand, France, the United Kingdom and the states of Hawaii, California and Florida in the U.S. have all adopted plans to deal with catastrophic risk. In Japan, New Zealand, and California the risk in question is earthquake. For France the main concern is flood. For Hawaii and Florida, the risk is hurricanes. For the U.K., the risk is terrorism.

Special Megacatastrophe Programs.

In the U.S., the states of Hawaii, Florida, and California have special programs to deal with megacatastrophes.

Hawaii. The Hawaii Hurricane Relief Fund works as follows: Insurance companies are allowed to write homeowners insurance with a hurricane exclusion. Each participating insurance company then acts as a servicing carrier for the HHRF, issuing the insured a separate hurricane policy and collecting a separate premium that is then forwarded to the HHRF. The HHRF receives ongoing revenue from hurricane premiums, insurance company assessments on property business, and mortgage recording fees.

The plan envisages providing insurance to cover a megacatastrophe costing up to $2.1 billion. This is over 1.5 times the cost of residential damage caused by Hurricane Iniki, which hit Hawaii in 1992.

Under the Hawaii scheme, the first 10% in loss from a megacatastrophe is assumed to be borne by homeowners through deductibles. The next loss layer would be paid by private insurance companies participating in the HHRF. The following loss layer comes from reinsurance purchased by the fund. The last $750 million comes from a line of credit, which is secured by future surcharges on all property/casualty premiums. If losses exceed the total coverage amount, claims are paid on a prorated basis. Coverage occurs when the National Weather Service announces a hurricane watch and ends 72 hours after the hurricane ends. The HHRF, however is now being phased out as private insurers have begun returning to the market.

Figure 5.6: HHRF - Claims Payment Funding Sources

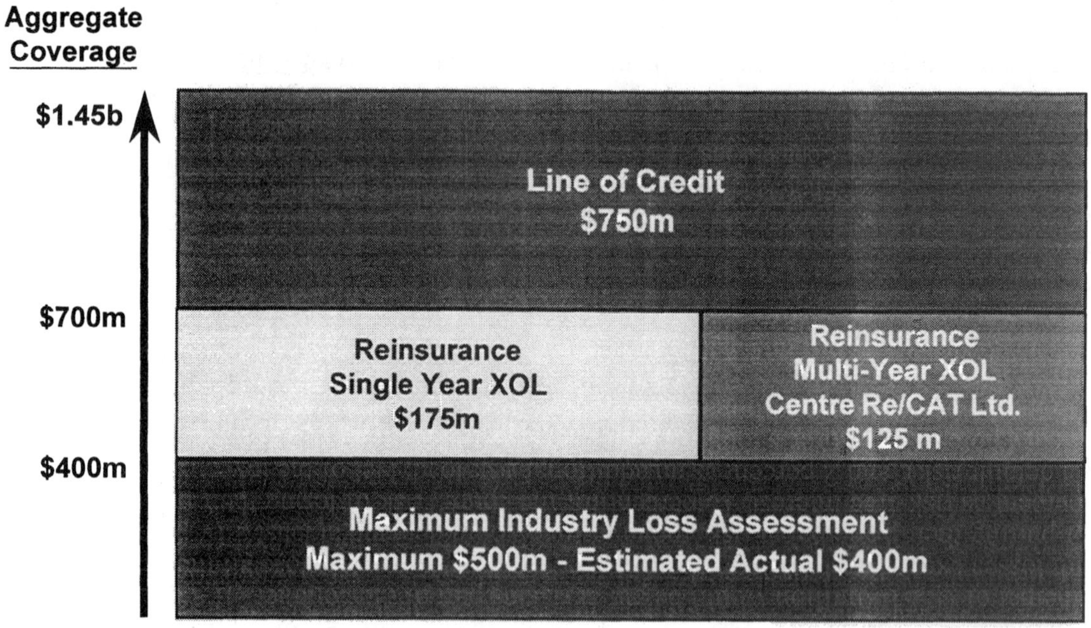

Source: Chase Securities

Figure 5.7: HHRF Source of Cash Flow to Pay or Finance Claims

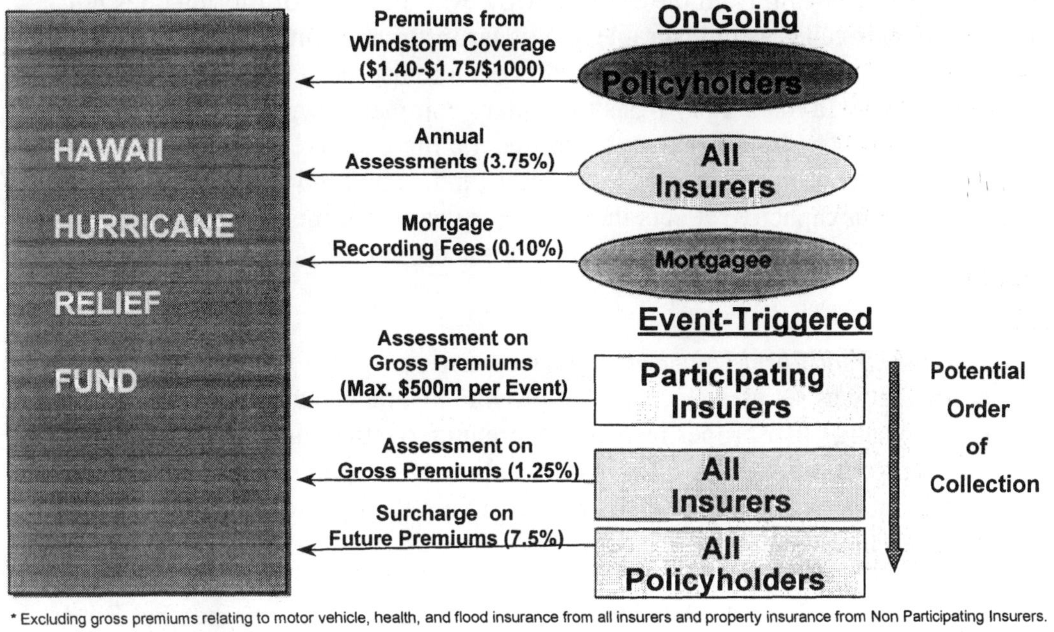

HAWAII HURRICANE RELIEF FUND

Premiums from Windstorm Coverage ($1.40-$1.75/$1000)	**On-Going** Policyholders
Annual Assessments (3.75%)	All Insurers
Mortgage Recording Fees (0.10%)	Mortgagee
Assessment on Gross Premiums (Max. $500m per Event)	**Event-Triggered** Participating Insurers
Assessment on Gross Premiums (1.25%)	All Insurers
Surcharge on Future Premiums (7.5%)	All Policyholders

Potential Order of Collection

* Excluding gross premiums relating to motor vehicle, health, and flood insurance from all insurers and property insurance from Non Participating Insurers.

Source: Chase Securities

Florida. Florida has a number of programs in place to alleviate the availability problems which developed in the state following Hurricane Andrew.

The state-run *Joint Underwriting Association* (JUA) is a property insurance pool that was set after Hurricane Andrew to provide homeowner multi-peril insurance to people who were having difficulty obtaining it. The JUA provides a market of last resort for comprehensive coverage, for policyholders in Florida who cannot purchase coverage in the private market. At its peak in 1996, the JUA had almost 1 million policyholders, a market share almost equal to the state's largest private property insurers. However, marketplace conditions appear to be improving. The various JUA incentive programs have been successful in attracting new insurers to the state and encouraging others to take on some JUA policyholders. With special incentive programs, various companies submitted proposals to depopulate the pool, a process that began in February 1996. Meanwhile, some of the state's largest residential property insurers are halting or limiting the sale of new policies, particularly for homes in the southern parts of the state and along the coast, and other insurers are not renewing some existing policies or requiring homeowners to purchase windstorm coverage from the windstorm pool.

The *Hurricane Catastrophe Fund* is a state-run catastrophe reinsurance program designed to encourage insurers to stay in the Florida marketplace. It was created following Hurricane Andrew in response to concerns about insurance availability. The fund, financed by residential property insurers doing business in the state (some 285 companies) based on their exposure to hurricane losses. It currently has a capacity of $11 billion for major hurricane claims, made up of about $3.1 billion in funds and $7.9 billion in borrowing capacity. The fund made payouts in 1995, although only minimally, with $9.5 million in claims payments for Hurricanes Opal, Eric and Allison.

The Florida reinsurance fund was created in an atmosphere where insurance companies were withdrawing from the market. However, the state of Florida does not regard the risk of hurricanes as uninsurable and so far insurance companies share this view. The Florida Hurricane Catastrophe Fund is not a reinsurer of last resort. The fund provides reinsurance on a mandatory basis to primary companies writing property insurance in the state. The fund is exempt from federal income taxes, which enables it to accumulate funds faster than would a private sector fund. The fund can borrow to pay losses. The borrowing capacity reflects the mandatory nature of the fund. It basically has the power to "tax" primary insurance companies and use the "tax receipts" to service debt.

The *Florida Windstorm Underwriting Association (FWUA)* is another state sponsored entity that was set up specifically to provide insurance against 'wind storm' risks for beach area and other properties which were under-served and where insurers were withdrawing from the market. The FWUA only insures against wind storm damages and thus encourages private insurers to maintain their presence in those coastal areas to cover other non-windstorm property perils.

The FWUA is a private association that is governed by a thirteen member Board of Directors, eight of whom are elected by member companies and five of whom are appointed by the Insurance Commissioner. Membership of the FWUA is mandatory for all licensed insurers writing property coverage in Florida. Pooling of windstorm risk in eligible areas allows the industry to continue to provide other coverages and spread the payment of windstorm losses over time. Member companies can also reduce their exposure to the FWUA by voluntarily writing coverage in the eligible areas.

The FWUA has immediate claims paying capacity equal to a 100 year probable maximum loss of over $5 billion. These claims paying resources include cash on hand, assessments that will be available from its members, reinsurance from the Florida Hurricane Catastrophe Fund, pre-funded bond issuance of $1.7 billion, and a $1 billion committed line of credit. The FWUA can pledge the assessments from members to borrow for loans or bonds that it is authorized to issue on a direct basis or through local governments.

California. The California Earthquake Authority began operating in late 1996. A state-run program funded in part by insurers, the CEA provides residential earthquake insurance. It was created by law in 1995 to ease the homeowners and earthquake insurance availability crisis brought about by fears of an earthquake more damaging than the 1994 Northridge quake which cost $12.5 billion in insured losses. The plan preserves the mandatory offer of earthquake coverage -- insurers who choose not to participate in the plan will be required to offer their own earthquake coverage to their homeowners policyholders. Under the plan, which needed the participation of 70 percent the market of California's homeowners insurers before it could start up, policyholders of participating insurers purchase earthquake coverage from the CEA. The CEA policy offers a scaled-down policy covering the home but not other structures such as swimming pools and garages. Contents coverage is limited to $5,000, and additional living expenses are capped at $1,500. The deductible on the home and on contents is 15 percent and is applied to the total loss, not separately for each coverage. Factors used to determine premiums include the location of the dwelling, the year it was built, and the type of construction. A 5 percent discount is applicable if the dwelling was built prior to 1960, walls are braced in a specified way, and hot water heaters are secured to the building frame.

The CEA has a funding plan structured in layers which totals $7.2 billion. The funding structure is as follows: the first $475 million in claims payments would come from the working capital of the participating insurers. These insurers would also be responsible for the next $2.15 billion in losses, which would be collected as assessments. The responsibility for the above sums will remain in effect for the next 10 years, so that if an earthquake causing more than $2.6 billion in damages does not occur within the first 12 years of the CEA's operation, insurers will be relieved of this layer of liability since the fund will have built up sufficient capital. In the event that a quake causes more than $2.6 billion in damage, an additional $1.4 billion in reinsurance payments will be available. The next layer will be provided by $0.7 billion which the CEA is authorized to borrow. This layer will be repaid through policyholder assessments totaling up to 20 percent of the earthquake premium. After these layers, $1.1 billion will be available as reinsurance from the Berkshire-Hathaway Insurance Group. The last $1.4 billion will be paid from assessments on participating insurers following an earthquake.

Statewide, earthquake coverage costs $3.91 on average for $1,000 of insured coverage. In low-risk areas of California, premiums would be $2 per $1,000. Residents in higher-risk areas, such as the San Francisco Bay region and some parts of Los Angeles, would pay premiums as high as $5.25 per $1,000, the highest rates allowed by the CEA. At these rates, the average Californian would pay $782 for $200,000 in coverage, but in the highest risk areas the same coverage would cost $1,050. However, because the rates are capped at $5.25, homeowners in the lowest risk areas subsidize those in higher risk areas.

New Zealand. In 1944, New Zealand enacted the Earthquake and War Damage Commission to cover "uninsurable risks." The program was extended over the years and now covers earthquakes, wars, flood, tsunamis, volcanoes and hydro-thermal activity. Properties are insured on an actual cash value basis, not replacement cost basis. The price for coverage is relatively low, at $0.5 per $1000 of fire insurance coverage.

The program can be viewed as successful in that it has been solvent and has been able to pay for a number of disasters that have hit New Zealand over the years. There is concern, however, in that the commission would not be able to handle "the big one" -- meaning a major earthquake in Wellington, estimated to cost over $2 billion. Of note, in 1990 the government of New Zealand made a raid on the fund for $239 million. This is a concern with all long-term funding mechanisms. As the fund builds and the money is not used, legislators may seek a way to use the funds for other purposes. The program is compulsory and does spread the risk over time, as it calls for the building up of a fund.

France. In 1982, the French government instituted a mandatory program to pay for floods and other natural disasters. A flat percent fee is charged on all non-life policies. Insurance companies then provide coverage for the specified perils. The insurance companies in turn can get reinsurance from the government-owned reinsurance company, Caisse Central de Reassurance (CCR). The program has been solvent, but there is concern that a major flood could exhaust its capacity which would require activation of the government guarantee and possibly triggering an increase in rates. The program is mandatory spreads the risk over time. Recently, the 1999 damages caused by windstorms Lothar and Martin as well as the Dordogne floods have largely depleted the CCR.

Japan. The Japanese earthquake program covering residential properties was established in 1966. Under the program, primary companies sell earthquake insurance. Homeowners are not required to buy the product and, since it is expensive, few do. The number of policies sold in 1994 totaled only 3.1 million, less than 10 percent of the market.

Primary companies reinsure their risk 100 percent with the Japanese Earthquake Reinsurance Company (JER), a government entity. The JER in turn retrocedes some of the risk to the private reinsurance market. The Japanese government provides the rest. In 1994, 85 percent of JER's exposure was with the government and 15 percent in the private market.

The program calls for high levels of coinsurance by policyholders. For example, in the case of a "half loss," meaning a loss between 20 to 50 percent of value, only 50 percent of the loss is covered by insurance. In addition, the Japanese government budgets each year a certain level of payment for the program. The current level is about $18 billion. If losses are higher, claims are prorated. For example, in the case of a $36 billion disaster, claimants would get only half of what they would receive for a disaster below $18 billion.

The Japanese program is not mandatory and hence there is low penetration. It should be emphasized that the underlying viewpoint in Japan is that the earthquake risk is basically uninsurable. This position is rarely stated explicitly, but the reality is that Tokyo is built in an active fault zone and a major quake could cause damage in the hundreds of billions of dollars.

Spain: Consorcio de Compensación de Seguros. Spain is exposed to a whole range of natural disasters namely earthquakes, volcanoes, windstorm, floods, hurricane etc but of all the hazards floods are the most severe cause of huge losses. It is interesting to note that the origin of the Consorcio is not related to losses due to natural disasters but losses as a result of riots during the Spanish Civil War from 1936-39. The way Consorcio handled the damages claimed as a result of civil war, was by issuing bonds which were accepted as cover for the technical reserves of the insurance companies. The repayment of the bonds was handled by imposing a surcharge which was levied on the premiums for certain classes of insurance (fire, theft and special covers) which had to be collected by the insurance companies and paid to the Consorcio.

The Consorcio is a State Organization, with its own legal status, full capacity to operate and capital independent of the State. One of the unique features of Consorcio is that it defines peril based on qualitative rather than quantitative aspects, that is, based on the enormous loss potential that they are likely to generate rather than providing protection conditional upon events occurring which affect either a very high number of insureds or a very wide territorial area. This eliminates the need for an event to be officially declared as a peril, as is the case in other programs, in the process minimizing subjectivism and accompanying delays in paying the claims.

Insurance covering extraordinary risks is obligatory under the system. The deductible is between 10-15% of the amount of the losses, depending upon the sums insured, but in no case shall exceed 1% of the sum insured nor be less than Ptas. 25,000. The primary source of funds to Consorcio is through its own premiums and surcharges. Given the risks, with high loss potential, that is being assumed by Consorcio and also given that it is a State Organization it is backed a State Guarantee.

Other Countries. Some countries have also introduced special insurance programs to cover acts of terrorism. In Northern Ireland, the program is strictly governmental. In England, a special program to cover acts of terrorism was put in place following two major explosions in central London in the early 1990s. Acts of terrorism are reinsured by a pool, "Pool Re," which can borrow from the Bank of England when its own resources are exhausted. South Africa has specific government programs to insure against property damage caused by terrorism.

Other U.S. Catastrophe Programs

In the United States, a number of programs are in place to address the issue of "uninsurable risks," meaning risks that cannot get coverage from the "voluntary market," that is, from private insurance companies. For property risks, 31 states have FAIR (Fair Access to Insurance Requirements) Plans. These Plans are mainly used to provide property insurance in inner cities. However, in a number of states they are utilized to cover other "hard to insure" exposures. For example, in California, the FAIR Plan covers homes exposed to brush fires and in New York the plan covers beachfront homes on Long Island.

Seven southern states have Windstorm Plans, which provide coverage for the wind peril alone. All of these plans (FAIR and Windstorm) operate by spreading the risk among insurance companies operating in the state. None is backed by the state government. In addition, each state has in place a guaranty fund to pay the claims of insolvent insurers. The guaranty fund is also supported by insurance companies with no guarantee or backup from the state government.

Market Assistance Plans (MAP)

Three states, New York, New Jersey and Texas have utilized Market Assistance Plans (MAPs) to provide coverage for shore properties. MAPs are voluntary mechanisms set up by the insurance industry in cooperation with the state insurance regulators to provide insurance when there is a "temporary" market failure. MAPs were utilized for the provision of liability insurance in the 1980s, where there was a short-term availability crisis for that coverage. In New York and New Jersey the viewpoint is that the current shortage of property insurance is temporary and affects only a small number of property owners. So rather than create a whole system to handle the problem, MAPs are used. In a MAP, companies volunteer to take on risks that are declined coverage in the voluntary market.

In Texas, which does not have a FAIR Plan, a voluntary MAP now covers more than 25 percent of the population and 427 zip codes. In addition, another initiative, the Property Protection Program, provides insurers with financial incentives to offer basic residential insurance coverage which can be tailored to fit the specific needs of people in inner city and rural communities as well as areas prone to severe hailstorms. The incentives are in the form of state premium tax credits and credits against assessments for the Beach and Windstorm Plan, known as the Catpool. This program is available in many of the same zip codes as the MAP. Companies representing more than two-thirds of the market are participating. The Insurance Commissioner is also requiring the state's Beach and Windstorm Plan to offer higher deductible options which range from 1.5 percent of policy limits to 5.0 percent. The new options percent went into effect in May 1996.

Linking Capital Markets to Emerging Economies' Risk Management Strategies

The above examples have shown how various jurisdictions and markets around the world have handled the problem of managing catastrophic risk. In most cases, these examples have addressed the needs of highly developed markets wherein the transfer of large risks has been accomplished with the participation of capital market players in those same markets. While small emerging economies subject to natural disasters may not domestically hold sufficient capital to absorb such risks within local markets, there is no reason why they should not have full access to the range of tools available from the international markets for risk management purposes. The above examples have shown that combining reinsurance, risk linked securities, and credit support, can provide more optimal mechanisms for financing and transferring catastrophe risks where they can be shared within larger pools of capital.

Governments and the private sector in disaster prone countries can and should exploit such mechanisms to the fullest extent in order to assure that national development is least affected by economic and financial shocks from such disasters. Multilateral institutions can help by providing the necessary credit enhancement and information transparency to link local risk management strategies with external risk markets. The next chapter, thus, more fully describes how such arrangements can be viably structured.

VI. FINANCIAL RISK MANAGEMENT PARAMETERS AND OPTIONS FOR A REGIONAL CATASTROPHE INSURANCE POOL

In the process of risk management, Caribbean governments and insurance companies need to implement a range of financial and policy tools to assure the optimal coverage of risks within budgetary and fiscal affordability limits. For risks which might have catastrophic consequences, the transfer abroad presents a key element in this strategy. However, the extreme of this approach without undertaking any domestic-based risk management efforts (in the financial and physical spheres) does not result in optimal catastrophe management practices in the long run, given the exposures to both catastrophic as well as insurance market risks. In addition, the traditional approach does not permit the effective development and strengthening of domestic insurance industries. Therefore, given the availability of regulatory strategies and financial instruments for risk management, the pooling of catastrophe risks at the regional level represents a comprehensive approach which resolves many of the structural problems experienced in the past. Pooling not only institutionalizes the coverage via insurance of catastrophic risks for both the private and public sectors, but also allows more standardization in the rating and pricing of such risks. As is discussed in this chapter, pooling also provides more leverage to cover risks with the limited capital available. By retaining some part of the risk which is bearable, this also helps stabilize the availability of such insurance funding and its pricing. This is accomplished via the more efficient accumulation of catastrophe reserves which can help buffer some of the global market risks related to natural disasters.

VI. FINANCIAL RISK MANAGEMENT PARAMETERS AND OPTIONS FOR A REGIONAL CATASTROPHE INSURANCE POOL

In this section, a financially feasible proposal for an ESC catastrophe insurance fund is analyzed. The section is designed to illustrate the concepts and challenges of creating such a fund, adapting the international experiences and market mechanisms to the ESC context.

Coverage for hurricane damage would begin for an island from the moment a hurricane watch is declared and end 72 hours later. Drawing the line in this fashion has the benefit of clarity. However, the definition could result in apparent inequities, particularly when an island is hit by a tropical storm which subsequently increases to hurricane strength and damages property on another island. The wind speed threshold (even if below hurricane strength) could therefore be defined a priori as a 'qualifying' event.

Insurance companies would sell the hurricane policy for the ESC fund, which would be a compulsory coverage, enforced by mortgage lenders. Premiums would be collected by the ESC fund and allocated in a two step process of reinsurance and financing. The financing would involve lending and capital markets which would provide a line of credit to the fund. In the event of hurricane damage above specified loss levels, the credit facility would be activated and funds provided to the pool. For illustrative purposes, let us assume that a standby credit to the fund totals $200 million. In the event of a hurricane costing, say, $500 million, and following the exhaustion of the available insurance and reinsurance capacity, the lender would disburse $200 million to the fund to pay claims for losses above reinsured levels. The fund, in turn, would then be repaid by industry participants of the region on a basis proportional to their hurricane loss exposure. Funds could be recouped by adding a tax or assessment to property/casualty insurance premiums, or imposing some other form of taxation as in the Hawaii Hurricane Relief Fund illustrated earlier.

To review the potential cost parameters of such a program, we initially assume that interest rates payable on sovereign risks in the ESC region are about 10 percent. However, if the fund came with a World Bank guarantee or loan facility, rates could be significantly lower. With a 15 year repayment period, principal plus interest amortization on the $200 million at the 10 percent interest rate would be $26 million per year. This is 0.2 percent of GDP in the ESC region, and would not constitute a major burden for the region's economies. As more hurricanes caused damage to islands, this cost could rise. However, based on the analysis of hurricane frequency, these costs would be manageable. It would also be feasible to create a layer of reinsurance coverage of over $500 million, so that damage from small but more frequent hurricanes could be covered without recourse to the financial markets.

Beyond the subsequent $200 million in financing, the ESC fund could purchase additional reinsurance if needed, up to the Estimated Expected Loss (EPL) level for the region if this was not yet covered and believed to be between $1.0 - $1.2 billion. For the sake of clarity in this first exposition, the EPL is assumed to be $1.0 billion.

The concept of creating regional pools for the purposes of reinsuring local primary insurers, has been debated often in the Caribbean. There are several options which can be considered in the design of regional pools, although key aspects to take into account are whether the creation of a pool gives incentives to primary carriers to reduce dependence on commercial international reinsurers solely for the associated commission income, and to what extent a pool itself will subsequently cede part of its coverage to international reinsurers (i.e., to optimize risk management). Both these issues will determine to some extent, the success and functionality of an insurance pool. The critical criteria should be the extent to which any pool arrangement is able to generate genuine additional capacity (see figure 6.1) rather than the reshuffling of existing capacity levels.

Figure 6.1: Catastrophe Risk Transfer Structure

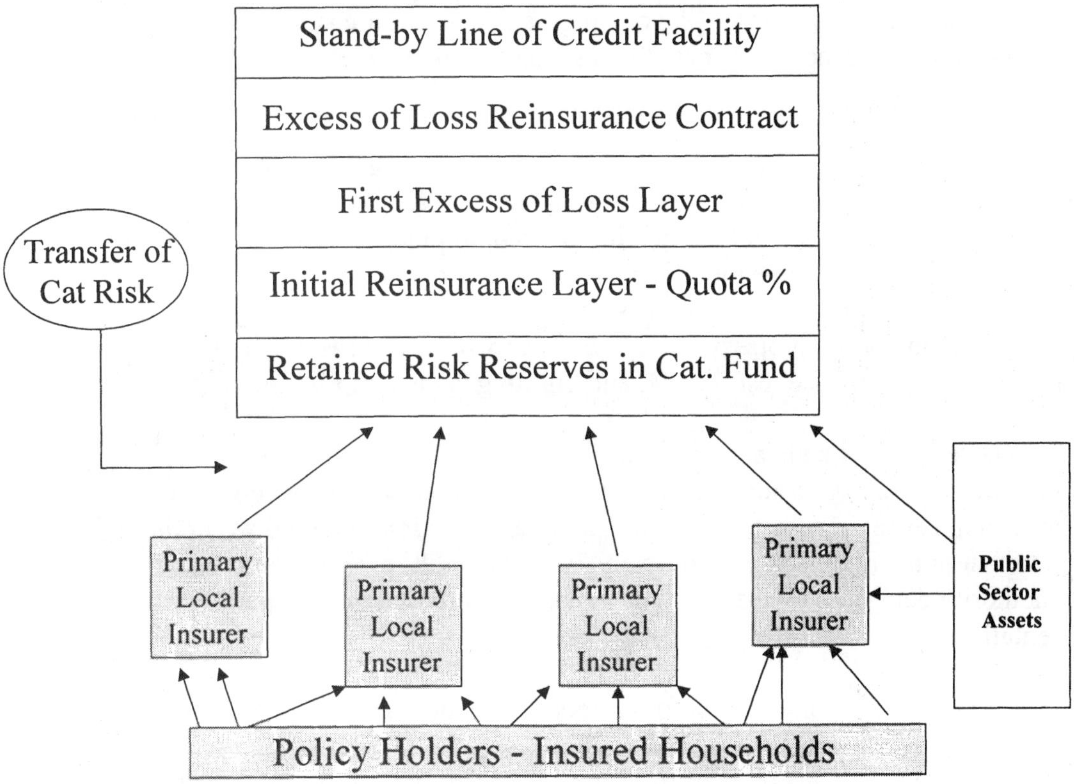

Source: World Bank

Reinsurance Pool and Risk Funding Arrangements

A key aspect to consider would be how the pool itself would retrocede[14] some of the risk to international commercial reinsurers and whether the pool would be a reinsurer at all versus a primary insurer for catastrophe risk. Sufficient initial capitalization and a minimum ongoing level of working capital would be required of the pool to assure that it retains sufficient coverage to meet its objectives. The result of

---

[14] 'Retrocession' refers to the reinsurance of an already reinsured portfolio. That is, property which is initially insured by a primary insurer, is then reinsured internationally and the reinsurer insures again (or retrocedes) the covered portfolio to yet another reinsurer. Some reinsurers that accept retroceded coverage, generally specialize in the catastrophe levels of coverage.

retroceding too much of its portfolio would likely invalidate much of the benefits of establishing a pool, unless of course, the excess of loss limits for such retrocession were at the higher levels of coverage, thus avoiding excessively high premiums and associated volatility. Reinsurers of course will also need to be convinced to take on any of the risks from a pooled portfolio at any level of coverage. However, this issue can be addressed by developing a priori, and providing, transparent information showing the derivation of the probable loss values of the pooled risks backed by methodologically robust techniques covering country-by-country and sector-by-sector risk assessments including damage and disaster event probability measures. In terms of private sector issues, there are very valid arguments for some of the large and secure carriers not to participate at all in the pool, thus depriving the pool from substantial premium income to maintain its operations. However, since this concern is in part due to the segmented quality of the regional market, it may be preferable to establish a pool for a smaller group of countries (e.g.: the OECS countries or a subregion excluding the larger countries) in which the insurance industry has fewer large players, regulatory norms are standardized, and where risk sharing would be much more beneficial given the small sizes and vulnerability of their national economies.

The pool should be administered by an independent party coupled with best practice underwriting and financial policies and should establish participation conditions for local primary carriers, including meeting prudential practices such as maximum limits for ceding coverage (i.e., some rational minimum local retention) coupled with minimum capital requirements and portfolio risk assessments based on a commonly understood methodologies (including property valuation, hazard zoning, disaster event frequencies, EPL methodology, land use restrictions, and building code compliance).

In terms of the financial management of a regional pool, its assets would be invested mostly overseas to achieve maximum returns and provide needed foreign exchange in the event of disasters. The management function of a pool would broadly equate to that of a large insurance company, with the pool's chief executive operating under authority delegated by the board of directors composed of pool participant representatives.

The initial full capitalization for regional pools or disaster reserve funds in line with actuarial requirements poses some funding risks, particularly with respect to the payment of claims. For this purpose, it is envisaged that during the early years of the establishment of any such fund, a multilateral institution might provide a guarantee of financing or a contingent line of credit for quick disbursement, if the pooled disaster fund assets are insufficient to provide the requisite upper level loss coverage for eligible indemnity payments. Alternatively, a pre-funded arrangement can be made by issuing long term bonds in the capital markets and making the proceeds available to the ESC fund (similar to that of the Florida Windstorm Underwriting Association discussed in the previous chapter).

A long term credit facility would be favorable in that it would be:

- committed or funded a priori.

- of longer term maturity thus lessening the repayment load.

- of lower financing cost than comparable commercial lines of credit due to a lower borrowing cost.

- less costly from an actuarial viewpoint, than reinsurance, at the highest potential loss layers.

The basic rationale for this approach is to better protect the Caribbean economies with improved risk management tools. Objectives are to diminish economic volatility in countries subject to shocks which are unrelated to international market movements, or where countries affected by single natural events are disproportionately affected. Key in this respect, is the need to reduce the level and volatility of catastrophe insurance premiums, and to increase overall coverage, given the inherent cyclical risks in the region. The objective would be to develop domestic financial industries and insurance-linked mechanisms which can help to increase the private sector capacity to better absorb and spread these risks.

In this context, the long term strategy is to ensure more sustainable development in the region by supporting development and implementation of risk sharing and risk transfer instruments that could adapt the latest risk financing and risk transfer technologies to the needs of the small Caribbean states. The objectives in this context would also include: (i) implementing more optimal risk transfer and institutional mechanisms to improve the efficiency and operation of insurance markets, (ii) providing liquidity for more rapid reconstruction in those cases where damage was incurred, including for the uninsured housing sector which is typically disproportionately affected, and (iii) reducing the vulnerability of structures through the improvement and enforcement of building code standards and land use/construction planning.

The proposed strategy to address these problems, takes into account the latest development in catastrophic risk transfer schemes, including those piloted by the natural disaster funds in Florida, Hawaii, California, Tokyo, and New Zealand. In addition, with the advent of the catastrophe options market developed under the Chicago Board of Trade, as well as the development of several weather indexed catastrophe bond instruments in the Reinsurance and Investment Banking industries, there are a number of innovative tools which could be adapted to the Caribbean context and result in much more optimal risk financing and risk transfer methods for coping with the severity and financial impact of natural catastrophes. The multilateral development bank role in this context would be to support the credit quality of such schemes as well as organizing and/or financing the appropriate technical assistance required.

Application of New Insurance Technologies

Two financial structures which are fully compatible both separately or as a unified mechanism, are proposed to address the challenges in the Caribbean. These are briefly described below:

Scheme 1: Liquidity/Credit Enhancement Facility to Support Property Insurance Coverage against Catastrophic Risks.

Objectives: (a) To increase the capacity of the insurance industry to absorb and spread such risks, (b) to augment coverage and protect/indemnify against property and business losses, and (c) to reduce the volatility impact of changes in international reinsurance pricing.

Financial Structure:

- The pool/fund would offer only catastrophic coverage to the general public, and would be channeled through local insurers for a management fee (insurance companies, however could purchase supplementary covers from the world market). The risks, however, would not be reflected on local insurers' balance sheets; they would be liabilities of the fund/pool itself.
- Catastrophic coverage under the fund is 'reinsured' by international reinsurers up to a specified loss limit.
- A multilateral development institution provides contingent credit at the next highest loss level, which also supports the liquidity of the pool/fund in the event of immediate large losses in the initial years of operation. Credit is eventually repaid/secured via future premium collections of the fund and, if necessary, surcharges or assessments. The long term loan/credit feature provides optimal risk spreading through time given the relatively long repayment period on the loan terms. This layer of 'cover' also buffers against the impact of fluctuation in international reinsurance pricing, given that loan terms (commitment fee, and/or interest charge if utilized) can remain relatively stable despite global market movements. Additional reinsurance can be purchased by the fund/pool above this layer as needed.
- If the fund/pool is majority private owned, the private investment arm of a multilateral development institution could help sponsor a private operator who would manage these pooled risks, but also avail itself of contingent support of the multilateral credit line (transferred on the same terms via the government) for liquidity assurance.
- Eventually, the liquidity support facility could be borne by the local financial markets with potential support from domestic and international commercial lenders. The multilateral institution would thus catalyze these instruments to allow domestic private sectors to engage in prudent risk spreading arrangements and lower the volatility of future economic losses.
- In exchange for the government's directing of multilateral institution proceeds to help fund the pool, the premiums collected for the pool would be assessed a minor charge/levy which would be paid into a separate trust fund for future disaster financing of low income households and crop damage to small farmers who were uninsured.
- With more stable premiums achieved, insurance cover would be compulsory for all middle income classes and households above a minimum income threshold.
- Proceeds from premiums received and retained in the fund, as well a the levy for the low income fund (above) would be invested in hard currency securities, to accrue additional returns.

As noted, the above structure utilizes a long term credit structure to both increase the capacity of catastrophic insurance coverage while cushioning the impact of large fluctuations in international reinsurance pricing. These typically occur following a series of major natural disasters around the globe. By putting in place a multilateral institution supported 12-15 year long term financing mechanism, this gives the scheme additional flexibility to finance more stable rates over time, because (i) the financed layer does not use reinsurance coverage thus insulating itself from market movements, and (ii) due to the long repayment period, rates can be kept more stable by spreading out the fund/pool's financial recovery period.

In addition, given the centralization of catastrophic coverage for the region, this would lead to further equalization and stabilization of prices over time. The structure depends on a government/industry partnership given that the government assumes some minor credit risk by passing on the long term lending terms to the insurance pool. However, the repayment of the credit would be structured so as to make future premiums and associated savings, a viable and reliable source of funds for such repayment, i.e., no government·subsidy is anticipated.

The second instrument proposed for development in the Caribbean region, is based on financial pay-outs linked to measurable weather events (or physical parametric triggers). The advantage of these instruments which can be structured under 'catastrophe bonds' is their relative ease of implementation once a reliable weather measurement mechanism is in place. Thus they bypass the traditional insurance loss adjusting function which requires evaluation of losses on a site-by-site basis before indemnity payment is provided. With parametric or indexed triggers[15], the payout is simply based on the index or physical parameter having reached a specific level or range, while the premium or spread is fixed in advance.

The main risk with weather indexed instruments is what is termed 'basis risk', i.e., the risk that the basis on which the loss payment is triggered (that is, the weather event such as a high windspeed or excessive rainfall) is not directly linked with the loss experience (e.g.: damage to a specific house or building). In other words, the event indexed instruments can have the risk that (a) payment is made (or the bondholder loses part of the bond payment) when the index is triggered even though no loss is experienced by the 'insured', or (b) a loss is experienced by the 'insured' party (e.g.: due to a lower than threshold windspeed) but the index is not triggered so no indemnity/relief is provided.

Given the proximity to the 'damage sites', it is more reasonable to expect that local insurers would take on this basis risk, while international reinsurers would generate the market in these instruments. The burden of the 'local basis risk' could also be shared the government, or alternatively the local insurers could purchase additional insurance to protect against such basis risk. The latter arrangement, however, would likely increase the cost of coverage to the ultimate customer, and thus make the scheme less attractive. Catastrophe bonds could also be triggered based on reported losses/indemnification claims in the industry rather than weather indexes, however, investor appetite might lessen without direct knowledge of local insurance industry characteristics, hence the attractiveness of the easily verifiable weather indexed triggers. The basic elements of such a structure are outlined below:

Scheme 2: Weather Indexed Catastrophe Bonds - Securitization of Catastrophe Risk

Objective: Establish easily measurable weather indexed insurance/bond contracts which would attract international investors given the risk-diversifying characteristics these have vis-à-vis global debt and equity markets, while permitting catastrophe risks to be spread into the broader capital markets.

---

[15] It should be clarified that "parametric" measures generally refer to physically measurable (parametrized) phenomena such as wind speed, rainfall, or earthquake intensity. The term "index" is usually used in the context of summarizing insurance/financial loss data across a certain region or a number of companies in the industry. In the case of temperature degrees, this can also be considered a special type of index since the temperature scale is a standardized measure. Similarly, with earthquake events, the Richter scale can be considered as a specialized index reflecting a number of factors contributing to that measurement. For risk securitization terminology though, direct physical data measurements are normally known as 'parametric' while the term 'index' is generally used for expressing aggregations of insurance dollar losses across a specified sector or region.

Financial Structure:

- A multilateral development institution would examine the possibility of sponsoring, with the assistance of international investment and reinsurance companies the development of 'catastrophe bonds' to be issued on domestic and international capital markets.
- The bonds which would pay higher than average yields have a risk of dropping their coupon rate and principal payments significantly in the event of a catastrophe (hurricane hit, major earthquake) to which bond payments are linked (e.g.: threshold windspeed or earthquake intensity).
- The multilateral institution would guarantee the payments of the bonds to investors, through a partial risk guarantee involving the government and the private bond issuer to ensure liquidity or contractual payments as scheduled.
- The domestic capital market would list the bonds on international exchanges to further transfer the risk into the global capital market. Since these risks are unrelated to typical stock market or other financial risks, they can prove attractive to international investors, and may provide them additional much needed diversity in their global portfolios.
- The bonds would trigger lower coupon interest payments and possibly partial principal losses upon the triggering of key weather events (e.g.: windspeed, earthquake intensity/magnitude).
- Trigger indicators would involve weather or storm indexes to be tracked via the installation in affected countries of weather station equipment with satellite links to 'recording centers', to track rainfall, windspeed, or other direct indicators of natural disaster adversity factors. These would serve as triggers for payout of such risk linked securities.

Prior to structuring such weather indexed ('parametric') bonds, data on weather events and associated losses would be compiled to ensure that a sufficiently strong correlation was achieved between the index-triggered payment and actual losses based on historical experience. Such data compilation is essential for the structuring and pricing of such insurance contracts. The key element of such contracts' success, however, is the reliability and objectivity of the weather measurement mechanism.

In the Caribbean, the Miami Hurricane (Tropical Prediction) Center provides substantial hurricane tracking data which could potentially be used in constructing the weather trigger source for such contracts. However, if such sources are not sufficiently 'fine tuned', particularly for small island areas, then a hard installation of 'on-the-ground' wind speed and rainfall measuring equipment may be necessary in the participating countries. Such hard installations would not be very costly, but would require telecommunication/radio linkages (e.g.: via satellite) to a central recording center to assure objectivity of the data reported.

From a portfolio management viewpoint, international investors would find it desirable to hold some of these instruments in their portfolio in order to diversify the usual financial market risks (ie.: achieve some non-correlation with global markets). While holding such instruments in their portfolio, they would of course be liable for potential losses or yield reduction in the event of a catastrophe. This income (as well as the risk of payout) would be factored into their overall portfolio investment return, though they would have the added assurance that a drop say, in the world stock or bond markets would have little or no effect on the performance of the catastrophe instruments during the life of the bond.

Combining Both Schemes in a Joint Structure and the Catalytic Role for Multilaterals

Due to the complementarity of both of the above schemes, the simultaneous development and feasibility testing of these would be essential, in order to best capture the range of catastrophe protection tools which might be applied in the Caribbean region. This would ensure the design of the most optimal pricing and risk transfer instruments within the limitations that domestic and external markets might bear. Participation of multilateral institutions would be crucial in the initial stages of this work, for the following reasons:

- Given the need for initial collection of economic, financial, and loss information, multilateral support would be essential to ensure objectivity and avoid perceptions of commercial ambitions by interested insurance, reinsurance or investment banking businesses.

- Some form of credit enhancement seems imminent even if a proposed scheme is considered fully financially viable. This is because multilateral institutions' leverage with governments to fulfill contractual commitments under the proposed schemes (e.g.: obligations to insurance companies, investors, trust funds for low income sector recovery, and average policyholders) would be a necessary confidence building measure to assure sustainability and avoid regulatory backsliding in the early years of implementation.

- The proposed schemes would not likely develop until sufficient liquid reserves were build up to protect both the liquidity and solvency of these structures. The multilaterals' longer term loans are ideally suited to 'protect' the financial integrity of the schemes during the initial years of operation, without causing undue financial stress on their solvency in the event of an early disaster event.

The weather indexed bond can be developed on its own as well as joining it with the first structure proposed, i.e., the insurance catastrophe pool with the liquidity/credit support layer. In fact, the weather indexed bond can constitute one of the upper layers of coverage in the pooling structure itself. In that manner, an alternative instrument for risk transfer can be added to the catastrophe fund/pool, which would involve investors financing some of the risk and thus further reducing the potential volatility of insurance/reinsurance pricing. In this manner, government properties could also be potentially insured at stable prices, and the local insurance industry could participate in coverage of broader sectors, in part through the use of the weather indexed instruments which could be deployed for hard-to-insure sectors such as small farming or public infrastructure. Besides international investors, domestic banks and capital market institutions could also help to add liquidity to the catastrophe bond market.

Financial support for the creation of these instruments separately or combined, would also have the objective of reducing the market failures which result in sub-optimal coverage due to: heavy fragmentation and scale diseconomies in the Caribbean property insurance market which increases the unfunded liabilities and costs of the industry, and lapses in prudent property coverage due to periodic premium rate hikes passed on by reinsurers (affected both by Atlantic hurricanes as well as other global catastrophe events). The international reinsurance industry would likely welcome participation in the form of such capital market/loan instruments as has occurred in the cases of Hawaii and Florida, as well as corporate specific instruments sponsored by Swiss Re., Residential Re., and other reinsurers to better manage and spread such risks.

Determining the Cost of Financing Catastrophic Risk

In order to adapt innovative risk financing instruments to cover insurable catastrophe risks, it is necessary to break out the components of such risks. The estimation of the following parameters rely on broad statistical distributions where the applicable coefficients are based on probability ranges using appropriate confidence intervals for specific 'reference event' estimates. The cost of financing catastrophic insurance risk can thus be defined as follows, where:

h = hazard intensity factor (e.g.: hurricane category/windspeed)
f = frequency probability of hazard
v = vulnerability factor of exposed property (structural vulnerability to hazard)
IV = insured value
EPL = estimated expected loss
d = damage ratio (equal to 'h' x 'v')

For example:

Assume that a frequency f of a hurricane in a given territory is once every ten years; this is expressed as 10% or 0.10.

The hazard h is a category III hurricane with weight given of 3 (or alternatively a similarly rated earthquake intensity).

The vulnerability coefficient of a given exposed property is 0.10; that is 10% damage will occur for each level of hurricane (e.g.: 10% damage for a category I; 20% for a category II, or analogous damage from earthquake intensities measured on the Richter scale).

Assume that IV the value of the insured property is $100,000.

The damage ratio d (based on a damage/severity function illustrated earlier) would then combine the vulnerability coefficient v with the hazard intensity h, so that:

$d = v \ x \ h$ or in this case $d = 0.10 \ x \ 3 = 0.30$

meaning that 30% of the property can be expected to be damaged from the hazard of the above cited intensity.

The estimated expected loss *(EPL)* therefore, would factor in the damage ratio d and the value of the property *(IV)*[16]:

$EPL = d \ x \ IV = \$30,000$

---

[16] However, on a portfolio basis, EPL can be significantly reduced since the hazard will not strike all properties in a portfolio in one 'hit'. International reinsurance companies take advantage of this diversity hedge, although Eastern Caribbean countries can also package their own risks and 'sell' them to international reinsurers with this hedge already built in.

The annual 'expected' *('EL')* average annual loss, or provision therefor, would thus take into account the frequency of the hazard and the *EPL* figure for the above property (calculated based on acceptable 'confidence' levels of statistical distributions for each hazard level and probability). Therefore,

$$EL = f \times EPL = f \times d \times IV \text{ or } EL = 0.1 \times 0.30 \times \$100,000 = \$3,000 = PP$$

The insurance company would therefore calculate a 'pure' premium (PP) of at least $3,000. However, the total premium is based on other factors as well:

$$PT = PP + exp + u + p + R$$

where:

PT = Total Premium (to policyholder);

PP = Pure Premium (as defined above);

exp = Expense component of insurance company (operating expenses, broker fees, business acquisition costs);

u = A risk load/uncertainty factor added to cover against less predictable catastrophic risks or those not fully captured by the above formula / projection;

p = A company's minimum profit margin / return on investment;

R = A primary insurance companies cost of reinsurance (i.e.: premiums paid for reinsurance minus commissions received from reinsurers).

The reinsurance component *'R'*, similarly is a function of a reinsurer's costs which have a similar cost structure to the primary insurers, albeit, with differing risk functions:

$$R = PP_r + exp_r + u_r + p_r + C$$

where: C = commissions paid to primary insurers for passing on premiums to purchase reinsurance cover.

Therefore, $PT = (PP + exp + u + p) + (PP_r + exp_r + u_r + p_r + C)$

However, the price of reinsurance *'R'* as can be seen, is not only based on actuarial projections covering hazard frequency, intensity, and vulnerability and value of insured properties, but also contains *'u'* the risk load uncertainty factor which for some reinsurers may simply be a hedge against bankruptcy and a required minimum return on their capital to protect against a miscalculation in the value of the pure premium *'PP_r'*.

In addition to these factors, the price of reinsurance at the higher excess of loss layers (see diagram below) is at times higher in proportion to the risk and chances of reaching losses at those levels. This increase in the "risk load" appears as a type of price 'stickiness' at those upper layers (which have a lower probability of being reached) and a fact that even if actuarial estimations yield lower 'pure premium' prices, the reinsurance industry nevertheless may charge proportionately higher in order to cover underwriting expenses as well as the uncertainty spread *'u'*

**Figure 6.2. Larger Risk Spreads in Reinsurance Prices
at Higher Loss Layers**

% probability of loss risk at $ value specified		Price of Insurance (premium rate) as % of expected loss
0.35%	Topmost reinsurance layer: for losses up to $140 mn. and above $120 mn.	3.5%
2.0%	Reinsurance for losses up to $120 mn. and above $90 mn.	5.5%
4.0%	Reinsurance for losses up to $90 mn. and above $60mn.	7.5%
10.0%	Reinsurance for losses up to $60 mn. and above $40 mn.	13.0%
15.0%	Primary Insurance up to $40 mn.	17.0%

Source: World Bank

The above example serves to show that while the probability of loss at the higher layers of coverage becomes lower (left side of diagram), the premiums charged, while lower at each level, nevertheless decrease at a slower rate. At the upper loss layers with lower probability, therefore, the premium becomes proportionately higher from an actuarial viewpoint. This is in part due to the 'uncertainty risk load' which is added to the high loss risk at these levels on top of the standard financial and administrative costs which become a larger share in the total premium. Because of this phenomenon as well as the potential reinsurance capacity constraints, use of alternative risk financing mechanisms for these event levels, become more feasible.

Applying these observations to the ESC market, the following is set out: Insurance premiums for the ESC are about $149 million per year, but these premiums cover routine losses like fire, as well as catastrophic risk. The average annual insured loss for catastrophes is therefore lower at approximately $90 million, based on the premium allocation of 60% in the region toward catastrophe risk coverage.

The lack of insurance for an estimated 30 percent of residents is a critical issue for multilateral development organizations. Following catastrophes, disaster aid would be much smaller and could be channeled in more productive ways if more insurance for rebuilding was in existence in East Caribbean nations.

The two major problems in the insurance system for ESC countries are: volatility and price. The price and availability of insurance is highly volatile, partly because of factors external to the ESC region[17].

---

[17] Marsh & McLennan Securities / Guy Carpenter, "The Evolving Market for Catastrophic Event Risk", August 1998.

Use of Contingent Credit as a Reinsurance Layer

Capital market initiatives not only include complementing traditional reinsurance with capital market funding, but also the use of risk financing, or credit support. Credit support has the advantage of lower costs if unused (i.e., a commitment charge only), but requires full repayment of principal and interest if used. Because of the latter reason, most primary insurance companies tend to stay with reinsurance contracts which, while requiring on average, higher annual payments of premiums, also provide full 'principal' protection or coverage in the event of a disaster. Nevertheless, where insurance capital capacity constraints exist (such as in the cases of Florida, Hawaii and California), credit instruments can supply that capacity and be repaid via future assessments on premiums. However, in tight insurance markets when premiums are high, the use of credit financing instruments can also be more cost effective if placed at the appropriate level of coverage. In this regard, the key variables and parameters to consider are the following:

Under the typical reinsurance contract we have:

R = cost of reinsurance to the primary insurance company

p = the frequency or probability (same as 'f' as defined earlier) of the hazard event

EPL = estimated expected loss

and we use the term 'r' to signify the risk free discount rate.

Therefore the expected annual flow to the primary insurer would consist of:

$$\frac{p\,(EPL)}{r} - \frac{R}{r}$$

that is, the expected annual loss $(p\,(EPL))$ minus the reinsurance premium R. Both factors are discounted by the risk free rate 'r', used to determine the present value of a perpetual annuity, that is, $R_{Pv} = R/r$. Assuming that both flows (the annual expected loss and the premium payment) can be normalized into a level amount per year, this would constitute a perpetual annuity for valuation purposes. Thus, for the primary insurer, the net present value of the reinsurance contract would be determined by the above (adjusted for secular changes in hazard trends and factors impacting the premium level).

Since the left side of the equation $(p\,(EPL)/r)$ will remain the same regardless of whether we utilize alternative risk transfer instruments such as contingent credit or not, then the comparison of the present value of the 'premium perpetuity' (R/r) must be made against the equivalent cost of credit. However, the cost of credit as discussed earlier is asymmetrical depending on whether the catastrophic event occurs or not. For these purposes, we define the following terms:

l_c = the loan commitment fee for maintaining a credit line in stand-by status;

l_r = the loan interest rate, chargeable upon disbursement of loan principal;

m = the period until maturity of the loan;

i = the ith period of repayment;

Therefore in comparing the cost of credit taking into consideration the actuarial estimates of catastrophe occurrence, we would express the present value of the annual cost of the credit as:

$$\frac{(1-p)(l_c(EPL))}{r} + \frac{p\sum_{i=0}^{m-1} ((l_r(EPL - (i/m)EPL) + |_{i=1}^{m} (EPL/m))}{(1+r)^i} \bigg/ r = L_{Pv}$$

In other words, in each year, the expected cost of the credit discounted from perpetuity equals: the non-probability *(1-p)* of the event multiplied by the product of the commitment fee and the estimated maximum loss (which in this case is used as the estimate of the required credit amount); plus the probability *(p)* of the event occurring, multiplied by the present value of the cost of the credit both in terms of interest and principal repayment. Again, the term *EPL* is used as the equivalent of the credit amount, and *i/m(EPL)* is the amount subtracted from principal outstanding each year for the purposes of calculating the interest amount due. Similarly, the term *EPL/m* reflects the principal installments payable assuming level payment of principal each year with no grace period. Prior to discounting the entire expression by '*r*' given the annual uniform expected 'annuity value', the expression is discounted by each period's risk free rate since each repayment of interest and principal carries with it a different relative present value.

The above principle of measurement is therefore used in this report to determine the cost effectiveness of utilizing alternative risk transfer and risk financing instruments *(L_{Pv} versus R_{Pv})* to complement traditional reinsurance, and in the process obtain a more secure and stable price for coverage which is possible with long term credit facilities. Using simulations over a 200-400 year period, and assuming a LIBOR cost of financing for credits with a ten year principal repayment period, risk financing becomes more optimal than reinsurance at specified event probability points. These are further elaborated below, however, for the purposes of testing feasibility, the 200 and 400 year elapsed periods are used instead of the 'perpetuity' since the former is more realistic in terms of "viable period sustainability". The reinsurance rates used reflect the current low rates for catastrophe risk – this becomes a very conservative assumption as rates appear to be at a cyclical low, and any increase in rates would result in more favorable outcomes for risk financing instruments.

Applying ESC Market Data to the Insurance Model

Property rates across the OECS, Barbados and Trinidad and Tobago vary considerably. This part of the region has three risk sub-zones, with the northern zone (Antigua and Barbuda, St. Kitts and Nevis) considered the higher risk area, the middle zone (Dominica, St. Lucia, Barbados) being medium risk, and the southern zone (St. Vincent and the Grenadines, Grenada, Trinidad and Tobago) being the lowest risk zone, particularly in terms of hurricane activity.

Table 6.1: Primary Insurance Rates for Residential Properties
Basis Points in Relation to Sums Insured - 1999

Antigua and Barbuda	120	(high risk)
Barbados	70	(medium risk)
Dominica	70	(medium risk)
Grenada	38	(low risk)
St. Kitts and Nevis	110	(high risk)
St. Lucia	60	(medium risk)
St. Vincent and the Grenadines	40	(low risk)
Trinidad and Tobago	35	(low risk)

Source: Insurance Association of the Caribbean, World Bank

Given the differentiated risk zones, sub-regional risk pooling would enable more optimal diversification of risk under a sub-regional insured portfolio which can then be more efficiently transferred to the reinsurance markets and/or the capital markets. Pooling of risks before reinsuring them lowers the aggregate portfolio's single event exposure thus reducing the capital carrying cost of funding catastrophe risk, or conversely, increasing the available capital for the same level of risk aggregated (see graph below).

Figure 6.3: Shift in Capital Supply Requirement
With Diversified Risk Portfolio

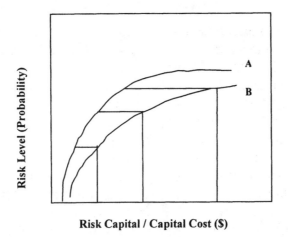

Source: World Bank

For the three risk sub-zones under a non-pooled scenario, curve B reflects the capital requirement with regard to the three risk level exposures individually. However, under a pooled and further diversified portfolio, the lesser risk capital required to cover catastrophe "hits" at any point in time over the entire portfolio, shifts the required capital supply curve back (curve A). Thus, at the same risk levels shown by the connecting horizontal lines, the risk based capital needed to fund the fair actuarial catastrophe risks becomes less reflecting a more efficient funding arrangement.

Risk Pooling

The following chart based on empirical data shows the reduction in the "portfolio" expected loss potential, as achieved through pooling of catastrophe risks. The chart is based on data collected on market values of private and public properties and assets, and types of construction in the ESC countries, and applies the historical hurricane intensity distributions and frequencies by individual country and country groupings in order to estimate expected "portfolio" losses as a percentage of total value, under pooled and non-pooled scenarios. The international reinsurance industry in effect already pools risks at a global level and thus achieves the lowest possible EPL coefficient in order to optimize the use of risk capital. However, while this practice is beneficial at the reinsurer level, it is conversely sub-optimal at the primary insurer level since proportionately more capital would need to be made available in a smaller more localized risk area such as a single hurricane prone island. In the East Caribbean, EPL percentages are in the range of 15%-25% with the average primary insurance company allocating its risk capital based on a 20% portfolio estimated expected loss or EPL. However, as seen earlier, reinsurers' EPLs are generally below 10%, and even in hurricane prone states such as Florida in the U.S., insurers' calculated EPLs are closer to 5% given the difficulty of a major hurricane hitting more than a fraction of the state at one time. The analysis below shows the EPL % loss as a function of the probability of various events of differing intensities, with the lowest probability shown to the right of the chart, reflecting an unlikely but very high intensity catastrophic event which corresponds to a higher EPL.

Figure 6.4: Effect of Risk Pooling on Loss Distribution Functions

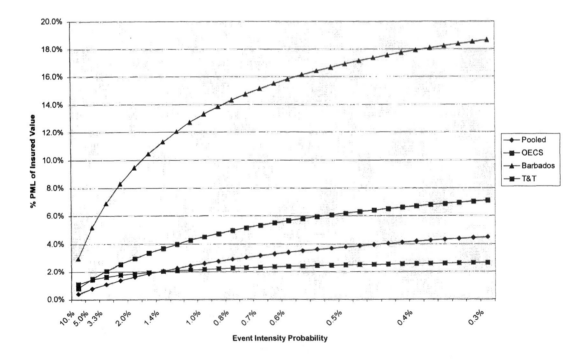

Source: Benfield Greig, Ltd.

As can be observed from figure 6.4, a single country such as Barbados which is rated similarly to medium risk hurricane prone islands such as St. Lucia or Dominica, has a much higher potential portfolio loss for all event intensities and probabilities. Even when the six OECS countries[18] which have roughly three risk zones (north EC, mid EC, and south EC) with the northern zone being most susceptible to hurricane losses, have their risks pooled under one portfolio, the potential EPL for the group of countries as one 'portfolio' is substantially reduced. Intuitively this is due to the fact that in any given year, the probability of one or more events affecting all of the islands simultaneously or within an annual time period, is highly unlikely. The pooling of risks to cover the broader region including OECS, Barbados and Trinidad and Tobago yields yet a lower risk profile for the combined pooled portfolio. The curve for Trinidad and Tobago risk remains the lowest in terms of loss exposure due the extremely low probability of hurricane events affecting that country.

Thus, the pooling of risks initially, before reinsuring them to transfer these risks abroad, has the benefit of requiring proportionately less capital for the same amount of risk, or conversely provides more available capital when moving from a segmented to a pooled arrangement. Additional capital has two benefits: (a) It permits more retention of risk thus providing more direct premium income to insurers and faster accumulation of capital, and (b) It permits reinsuring risks at higher loss levels where premium prices under XL contracts are cheaper.

The following chapter quantifies the gains obtained from insurance pooling and sets out the financing structure of a regional catastrophe insurance pool supported by alternative risk financing instruments which are tested against the costs and benefits of catastrophe reinsurance contracts. Based on this analysis, the feasibility of establishing a regional catastrophe pool with the participation of the insurance industry and the insurance of government assets, is demonstrated. The use of contingent credit at the uppermost levels of potential loss, is also tested in order to provide an optimal combination of retained capital, reinsurance risk transfer, and credit backstop support to finance catastrophic risks more efficiently.

---

[18] Antigua & Barbuda, Dominica, Grenada, St. Kitts & Nevis, St. Lucia, and St. Vincent & the Grenadines.

VII. INSURANCE POOLING WITH ALTERNATIVE RISK FINANCING INSTRUMENTS FOR CATASTROPHIC RISK MANAGEMENT

The demonstration from a financial feasibility view, of the benefits and sustainability of a regional pooled structure must take into account not only expected claims but also the income and expense flows of both insurers and reinsurers. In this regard, the proposed pooling approach would increase insurance coverage in the ESC while maintaining or increasing the net income of both insurers and reinsurers, a pre-requisite for participation backed by appropriate economic incentives. Since pooling permits increased funding of risk with proportionately less capital, this generates efficiencies in terms of leverage in using reinsurance as well as alternative risk financing instruments. At the same time, domestic insurers' bottom line is unaffected since the pooled structure allows them to retain additional non-catastrophic risks which permits greater retention of gross premiums collected. From the reinsurance standpoint, transaction costs of reinsurance treaties are reduced and the inclusion of public assets increases their share of coverage while providing more favorable terms due to the proportionately lower reinsurance requirement of the pool. Alternative risk financing instruments such as credit backstop facilities and catastrophe bonds are tested, to show that these can positively complement pooled insurance/reinsurance structures by providing cost effective multi-year coverage which allows stabilization of pool premiums and available capacity.

VII. INSURANCE POOLING WITH ALTERNATIVE RISK FINANCING INSTRUMENTS FOR CATASTROPHIC RISK MANAGEMENT

Following the quantification of insurable assets at risk, and the actuarially estimated loss exposure parameters on both a pooled and non-pooled basis, the next step is to determine the financing and capital structure of a catastrophe pool which would increase the leverage of domestic capital, while optimizing risk transfer and financing arrangements for coverage of disaster losses. In this context, this section starts by estimating the required risk capital for an insurable asset base (including public sector assets), and proceeds to test feasibility and sustainability of such a pool including use of cost effective credit backstop facilities to finance losses at the upper (lowest probability) levels.

The insured assets in the ESC have been estimated to be valued between $18 - $28 billion. A method for confirming current estimates of the insured value of assets, is utilizing the following figures reported as gross premium for all property insurance classes:

Table 7.1: Gross Property Premiums – ESC Area

Country	Premiums US $ mn.
Antigua and Barbuda	10.6
Barbados	43.0
Dominica	3.8
Grenada	8.6
St. Kitts and Nevis	9.0
St. Lucia	11.9
St. Vincent and the Grenadines	9.6
Trinidad and Tobago	52.1
Total	$148.6

Source: Insurance Association of the Caribbean.

Using the weighted average premium-rate per sums insured, of 0.59 % across all the countries listed, the total insured assets for these countries in aggregate are estimated to be $25.13 billion which, based on independent value estimates, would represent the high end of the range of total market values of properties in the region.

The average Estimated Expected Loss (EPL) ratio of 20% of total values insured for the region ($25.13 bn.) , would thus imply an insurance liability funding requirement (premium reserves plus capital and/or supplemented by reinsurance) of $5.03 billion.

A catastrophe pool, however, would only attempt to cover the 'cat' portion of the risk which pertains to 60% of the total coverage based on the premium breakdown.

However, before applying this portion of the risk, one must take into account the reduction in EPL provided by the pooled structure. As the previous analysis shows, the Barbados/OECS/Trinidad and Tobago pooled structure would provide an aggregate portfolio EPL of only 5% given the diversification of risk and annual expected losses of the pool as a whole, versus expected losses for individual countries (based on historical frequency event and loss data). Therefore, the above estimated funding requirement of $5.03 billion adjusted for the 60% 'cat' portion would amount to $3.02 billion. If, however, one utilized the pooled EPL of 5% over the aggregate of $25.13 billion adjusted for the 'cat' portion, this would result in a net insurance capital requirement of $25.13*0.60*0.05 = $0.75 billion or $750 million.

The difference between the higher EPL estimated capital requirement of $3.02 billion minus $0.75 billion equals $2.27 billion in surplus available capital on account of pooling. Since the current practice is to reinsure under proportional treaties a share of approximately 70% of gross written premiums as well as another 20% of the remaining 30% reinsured under XL contracts, this results in a typical net retention by primary companies of (100% - 70%) – 20% = 24%. Thus, if reinsurance arrangements under the pool were the same as for the local industry, this would result in a minimum pool retention of $0.180 bn. (24% * $0.750 bn), or a reduction 'saving' of $0.545 bn. versus the non pool retention amount of $0.725 bn. (for catastrophe risks only).

Under the non-pooled situation, the retention after using XL cover, or 24% net, would have been referenced to the cat portion of coverage of $3.02 billion, that is, the $725 million of the retained requirement which would be required under current practices. However, the "risk savings" of $545 million in net capital on account of the lower EPL in the pool can also be used for additional primary risk retention. Thus total risk retention under the pooled scenario could amount to $0.725 bn. instead of $0.180 mn. ($0.725 mn. - $0.545 mn. = $0.180 mn.) without an increase in risk but with the potential to take on increased insurance coverage. The additional capital at the retained pool level would not only imply additional gross premium income (without a reinsurance cost), but would also permit faster accumulation of pool reserves.

Primary insurers in the region could still benefit from an available increase in the retention of 'non-catastrophe' risks, in an amount at least equal to the $0.725 mn. transferred to the pool for 'cat' risk. Any non-cat retention beyond that level would accrue as additional gross premium income at a rate of $PT_i*(1 - C_{nc})$, where PT_i is the incremental gross premium collected, and C_{nc} equals the percentage commission which would have been received if the risk had been ceded to reinsurers. As described further below, the retention of 'non-cat' risks and associated premiums can be increased substantially given that, in the absence of catastrophe risks on the balance sheet, this presents companies with significantly more manageable insurance liabilities.

An additional benefit of higher risk retention by primary companies is that using less protection at the more frequently used lower levels of cover, would shield them from international rate fluctuations which at those layers have more frequent impacts on company balance sheets since those such layers of coverage are invoked more often.

Table 7.2: Financial Parameters Under Pool and Non-Pool Scenarios

(US $ billions)	Pre-Pool Scenario (i)	Pool Scenario (ii)
a. Total Sum Insured	25.3	25.3
b. Gross Premium	0.149 (0.59% of 'a')	0.149
c. Est. Expected Loss	5.03 (20% of 'a')	1.265 (5% of 'a')
d. Catastrophe Portion	3.02 (60% of 'c')	0.75 (60% of 'c')
e. Capital Requirement	3.02 (= $d_{(i)}$)	0.75 (= $d_{(ii)}$)
f. Pool Capital Saving	---	2.27 ($e_{(i)}$) – ($e)_{(ii)}$
g. Net Retained Capital	0.725	0.180 to 0.725
h. % of Cat Risk	24% ($g/d_{(i)}$)	24%-97% ($g/d_{(ii)}$)

Source: World Bank

Under the above scenario, therefore, ceding the catastrophe risk of primary companies to a pool, would increase the capital leverage of the pool and result in more efficient reinsurance arrangements. However, mechanisms would be needed to ensure that cession of the 'cat' risk would not result in lower overall financial results. This can be achieved via two instruments: (a) replacing some of the reinsured non-cat risks with additional risk retentions, and (b) expanding the non-cat risk portion of the underwritten portfolio (e.g.: by underwriting residences, small commercial, and public sector assets). In addition, it would be expected that primary insurers would still receive commissions on their cat risk premiums transferred to the pool, although the commission rate might vary given that cession to the pool would imply a direct transfer of risk versus reinsurance proper. Nevertheless, primary companies would still be expected to service policy holder accounts and thus a reasonable commission would be warranted.

The existing underwriting arrangements as at present (pre-pool) reflects the following insurance/reinsurance structure:

Figure 7.1: Insurance/Reinsurance Premium Structure of the Eastern Caribbean, Barbados and Trinidad and Tobago (cat and non-cat risks)

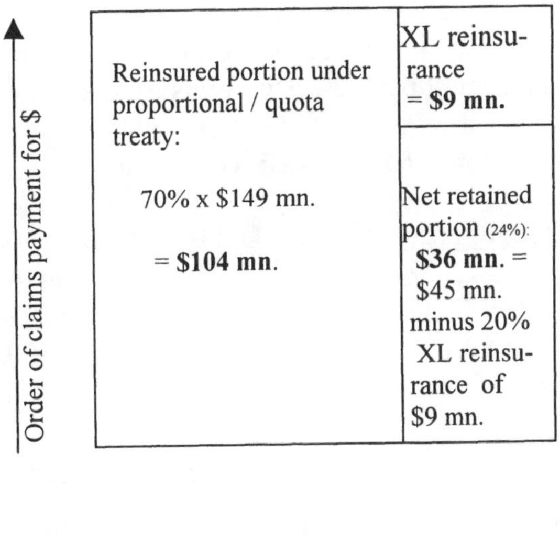

Source: World Bank

By ceding the *catastrophe* portion of the initially retained premiums (i.e., $27 mn. = 60% x (30% x $149 mn.)) of the total before XL reinsurance, this would leave a remainder of $18 mn. of retainable premium for the primary insurers. Since XL cover would no longer be necessary (as the cat risk would be handled by the pool), the primary companies would end up with a resulting retained portion for all risks, of $18 mn. = $45 mn. - $27 mn., versus $36 mn. as in the present situation above. However, the reduction from ceding the 'cat' risk (which would nevertheless still provide some commission income) could be 'compensated' by reducing the remaining non-cat risk currently reinsured under the quota treaty, and increasing the corresponding retention:

**Figure 7.2: Insurance/Reinsurance Premium Structure
After Ceding Catastrophe Risk to Pool
and Reducing Remaining Proportional Reinsurance**

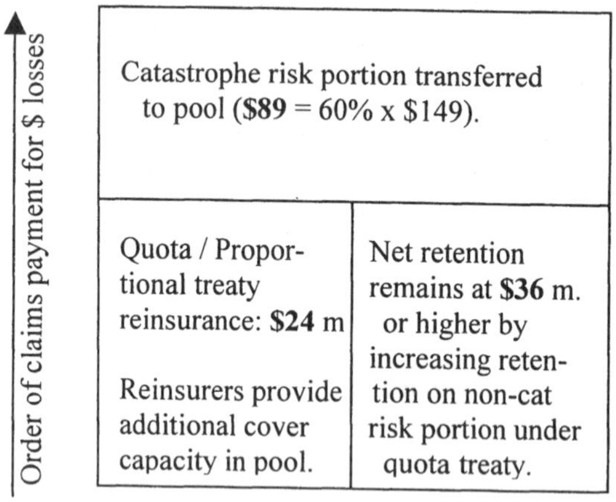

Source: World Bank

Inclusion of Public Sector Assets and Other Uninsured Properties

In addition to the restructuring of catastrophe insurance arrangements as per above, primary companies can also augment their non-cat portfolio by insuring public sector assets and currently non-insured households, assuming a supportive regulatory framework for compulsory catastrophe insurance protection. Estimated public sector assets , uninsured households and small businesses in terms of total value, are as follows:

Table 7.3: Exposed Asset Values

	Government Assets	Uninsured Households/Businesses
OECS	$2,172 m.	$414 m.
Barbados	$836 m.	$298 m.
Trinidad and Tobago	$2,161 m.	$350 m.
Total	$5,169 m.	$1,062 m.

Source: World Bank, Benfield Greig

In the above figures, government assets include public buildings, government buildings, utilities, ports, airports, roads, schools, hospitals, and other public sector assets. Adding in the above assets totaling almost $6.3 billion and using an average but conservative premium rate of 0.6% of insured value would result in additional premium volume of $37 million of which the catastrophe portion would constitute $22 million and the non-cat portion $15 million, and assuming transfer of all catastrophe risks to the pool, the following premium structure would result in the following:

Figure 7.3: Insurance/Reinsurance Premium Structure after Ceding Catastrophe Risk to Pool and Adding Government Assets and Non-insured Homes

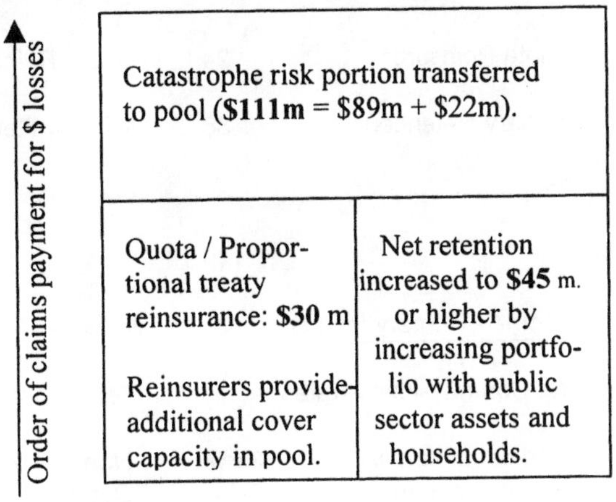

	Catastrophe risk portion transferred to pool (**$111m** = $89m + $22m).	
Order of claims payment for $ losses →	Quota / Proportional treaty reinsurance: **$30 m** Reinsurers provide additional cover capacity in pool.	Net retention increased to **$45** m. or higher by increasing portfolio with public sector assets and households.

Source: World Bank

Under the above arrangement, primary risk retention would increase to 60% since this reflects purely non-cat risk. The table below shows the financial results for insurers and reinsurers alike for the transition from current arrangements to the proposed insurance premium structure utilizing the pool for catastrophe risk cover (figures in $ millions except where indicated):

Table 7.4: Insurer Financial Results in Pool and Pre-Pool Situations

Current Situation		Initial Pool		Final Pool	
Quota Reinsurer	104	Quota Reinsurer	24	Quota Reinsurer	30
Primary Retention	36	Primary Retention	36	Primary Retention	45
XL	9	Pool	89	Pool	111
	149		149		186
Income - Primary Insurer		**Income - Primary Insurer**		**Income - Primary Insurer**	
Re. Commissions		Re. Commissions / Rates		Re. Commissions / Rates	
Non-cat comm. %	0.33	Non-cat comm. %	33.0%	Non-cat comm. %	33.0%
Cat comm. %	0.22	Cat pool comm. %	15.0%	Cat pool comm. %	15.0%
		ROL 40%-60% layer	4.5%	ROL 40%-60% layer	4.5%
		ROL 60%-80% layer	3.5%	ROL 60%-80% layer	3.5%
Non-cat commission	13.73				
Cat commission	13.73	Non-cat commission	7.92	Non-cat commission	9.90
Net premium income	36.00	Cat pool commission	13.35	Cat pool commission	16.65
Total	63.46	Net premium income	36.00	Net premium income	45.00
		Total	57.27	Total	71.55
Income - Reinsurer		**Income - Reinsurer**		**Income - Reinsurer**	
Premium - commiss.	76.54	Premium - commiss.	16.08	Premium - commiss.	20.10
		Pool Quota Re 20-40	12.10	Pool Quota Re 20-40	15.10
		Pool XL (40-60%)	23.08	Pool XL (40-60%)	28.78
		Pool XL (60-80%)	16.89	Pool XL (60-80%)	21.07
		Total	68.16	Total	85.05

Source: World Bank

The total income increases for both insurers and reinsurers in the final pool structure, on account of higher non-cat retention by primary insurers and additional reinsurance coverage provided by reinsurers under the pool. Commissions and reinsurance prices used, are shown under the 'Re. Commissions / Rates' section. For the pool structure, the reinsurance arrangements used assume a structure whereby the first 20% cover is retained in the pool, the second 20% uses a proportional quota treaty with 20% co-insurance, and the third and fourth 20% layers use XL coverage. The last 20% layer is assumed to be funded via a backstop credit line. The above therefore, shows the elements of insurance income which affect the respective parties under each of the structures shown. As the pool built up funds, the retained capital would rise accordingly. The implied pool structure, in terms of premium distribution, would thus be as follows:

Figure 7.4: Implied Pool Structure for Allocating Catastrophe Risk Premiums

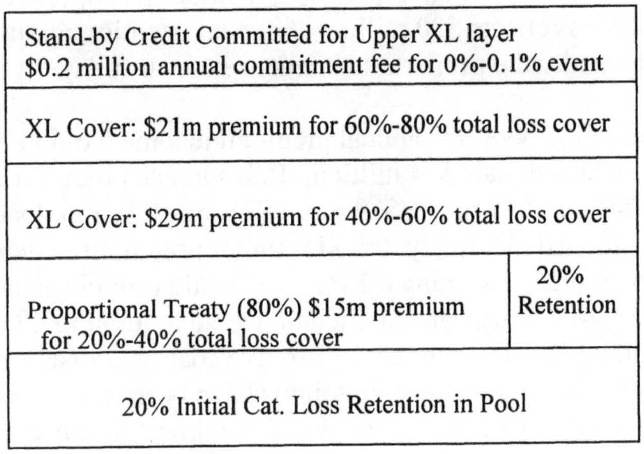

Stand-by Credit Committed for Upper XL layer $0.2 million annual commitment fee for 0%-0.1% event	
XL Cover: $21m premium for 60%-80% total loss cover	
XL Cover: $29m premium for 40%-60% total loss cover	
Proportional Treaty (80%) $15m premium for 20%-40% total loss cover	20% Retention
20% Initial Cat. Loss Retention in Pool	

Source: World Bank

And the consequent distribution of funding mechanisms by the corresponding loss levels would be:

Figure 7.5: Implied Pool Capital Structure for Financing Catastrophe Losses

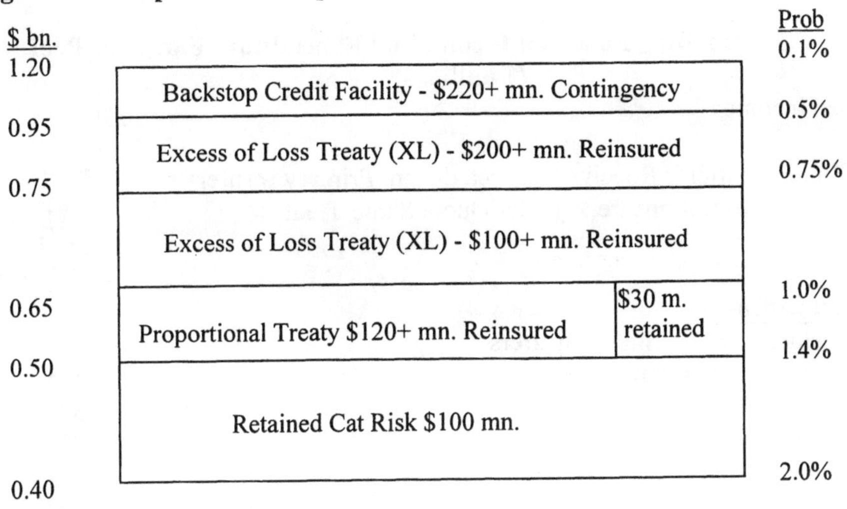

$ bn.		Prob
1.20	Backstop Credit Facility - $220+ mn. Contingency	0.1%
0.95	Excess of Loss Treaty (XL) - $200+ mn. Reinsured	0.5%
0.75	Excess of Loss Treaty (XL) - $100+ mn. Reinsured	0.75%
0.65	Proportional Treaty $120+ mn. Reinsured / $30 m. retained	1.0%
0.50	Retained Cat Risk $100 mn.	1.4%
0.40		2.0%

Source: World Bank

Since the retention level is substantial and amounts to a 'deductible' for any particular event, this layer can be structured in separate 'cylinders' per country so that each country's exposure has the same benefits of the pool structure for its proportion of the retention:

Figure 7.6: Structure of $100 mn. Retention Layer by Country

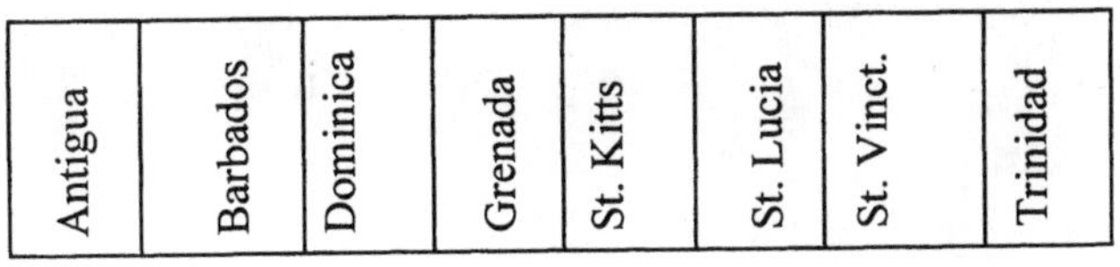

| Antigua | Barbados | Dominica | Grenada | St. Kitts | St. Lucia | St. Vinct. | Trinidad |

Source: World Bank

Thus, for example if St. Lucia's portion of the retention layer was $10 million, and the country suffered a loss totaling $30 million, it would be eligible to collect $16 million from the pool. This reflects $20 million above its retention minus the 20% co-insured retained portion under the proportional treaty reinsurance layer.

At the initiation of the pool, the annual premium income would be $111 million less 15% commissions which equals $94 million. Reinsurance premium costs to the pool would amount to $67 million ($15 mn. + $29 mn. +$21 mn. + $2 mn. loan commitment fee). However on the proportional treaty, the $15 mn. of premiums ceded would accrue a commission to the pool, which, assuming a 15% rate, would provide an additional $3 million. Therefore, the pool's initial annual income would amount to $97 million, leaving a surplus of $30 million to cover administrative costs and to accumulate reserves. It should be noted that the XL reinsurance premiums have been 'conservatively' estimated at rates which are actuarially fair but are three times the current market rates, to take account of potential future price fluctuations and potential variations in the estimated expected loss percentage. Therefore a significant cushion exists for additional savings if these 'adverse' events do not develop. Nevertheless, since the pool assumes a retention of at least $100 million in cat risk, this amount would be required as initial capital. This could be provided by private sector shareholders, strategic investors, or other means.

Table 7.5: Resulting Financial Income and Expenditure Flows for Pool
($ millions)

Financial Income

Catastrophe Premiums Received collected from Primary Insurers	$111
Commissions from Reinsurers (under Quota Share Treaty)	$3
Total	$114

Financial Expenses

Commissions paid to primary insurers	$17
Net Quota Share premium paid	$15
XL first layer premiums	$29
XL second layer premiums	$21
Credit commitment fee	$2
Total	$84

Net Income/Flow	$30

Source: World Bank

Defining a Catastrophe Pool for Public Assets

While the above analysis has combined both public and private sector assets in the pool structures as defined, governments could also choose the option of establishing a purely government pool to insure public assets and infrastructure. While such a pool would have less capital than the combined private/public pool, it could nevertheless be considered as an option if inclusion of private insured assets proved to be unwieldy or less desirable to the domestic insurance industry even if it implied no reduction in net income flows. Below, a potential structure for a sub-regional government insurance pool is outlined as well as the financing role of multilaterals in order to assure initial liquidity for the pool and provide a topmost layer of excess-of-loss protection in case of a major catastrophic event.

The pool described would follow the same financial structure of the industry/public assets pool described above. The assets included in the pool would be government buildings and properties, schools, hospitals, and critical infrastructure facilities such as electricity and water transmission systems. A key aspect to consider in a public asset insurance pool, is each government's tolerance for the payment of premium from its fiscal budget. Therefore, such a structure would first need to determine the level of premium 'subscriptions' for a specified range of assets, commensurate with the affordability constraints and risk management objectives of each government.

An additional feature of a government assets pool would be the provision of a low layer credit line from the World Bank or other multilateral agencies, to protect the pool from losses if they occurred early in the cycle before the premium build-up provided a sufficient capital cushion to absorb risks before reinsurance layers were invoked. This lower end protection becomes more feasible in a government versus a private sector pool since the credit line becomes a public 'general' liability while in a private sector pool such a liability at the lower layer could constitute too high of a debt burden for corporate statutory standards. However, in the public sector case, since losses at the subsequent layer would be covered by reinsurance, the debt burden is strictly limited to the difference between available capital for 'retained' risk and the required full retention amount before the reinsurance could be invoked.

Figure 7.7: Outline of an Insurance Pool Structure for Public Assets

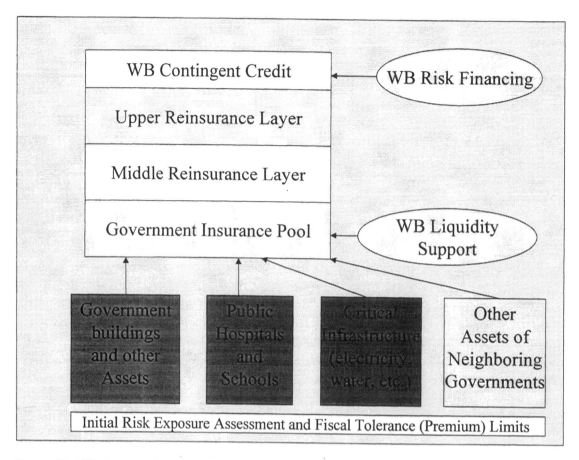

Source: World Bank

The structure also includes a top layer risk financing facility as in the private sector pool, which would only be invoked at the lowest probability event levels which generated losses above the last reinsurance layer. As will be shown in the next section of this chapter, such financial instruments prove to be more cost effective in the long run than adding an additional topmost reinsurance layer, since they require little or no cost when not deployed, and they allow repayment over a long period when used (which can be funded by future premiums).

Results Obtained from Testing Risk Transfer and Risk Financing Mechanisms

This section provides the methodology and results for testing viability of alternative risk transfer mechanisms for financing catastrophic risks. Capital market products such as loans of different maturities and pricing (commercial, IBRD, IFC) were tested for specified event probabilities, and compared with existing available reinsurance pricing. Commercial loan financing was tested utilizing credit enhancement instruments such as the IBRD Guarantee which was also used to test viability of catastrophe bond products for capital market issuance.

Event scenarios at the 5% probability level (reflecting relatively frequent but less loss intensive hazards) were first tested over a 200 year simulation period using IBRD loan terms of 15 year maturities and 5 years grace at an interest rate of 6.5% (above the current IBRD variable rate). The market premium for excess of loss reinsurance at this level is 7-8% of the loss layer covered, though a 7% rate was used. The same exercise was also applied to IFC loan terms using a 10 year maturity, 2 year grace, and an interest rate of 10.5% reflecting the high end of IFC pricing which ranges between LIBOR + 2 to LIBOR + 4. Commercial credits were also tested using maturities of 6 years with 1 year grace at 11% interest cost. A 5% risk free rate was used as the discount factor. This rate is extremely conservative and tends to bias results in favor of reinsurance cover when compared to utilizing an opportunity cost of capital rate which might be double the risk free rate and which would tend to bias results towards credit instruments.

For commercial financing, an IBRD guarantee was assumed in order to provide credit enhancement for private sector lenders to participate. The type of guarantee is not specified because both a partial credit guarantee would apply (e.g.: to ensure a minimum maturity period of the loan or loans) or a partial risk guarantee (to ensure contractual commitments on the debt service obligations). In both the cases of risk transfer (reinsurance) versus risk financing (lending), the net present values for the "insured" were negative, that is, after taking into account the indemnity payments received following a disaster, the policy holder or primary insurer would not "profit" from the coverage, which is consistent with the use of insurance for protecting against cash flow shocks and drastic reductions in asset wealth. The results are as follows:

Table 7.6: Testing Alternative Risk Financing Instruments: IBRD, IFC and Commercial Loan Terms Using 5% Catastrophe Event Probability

	Reinsurance	IBRD Terms	IFC Terms	Commercial
Simulation period	200 years	200 years	200 years	200 years
Event probability	5%	5%	5%	5%
Premium Rate	7%			
Interest Rate	na	6.5%	10.5%	11.0%
Commitment fee	na	0.75%	0.5%	1%
Front end fee	na	1%	1%	1%
Maturity/grace	na	15/5	10/2	6/1
Guarantee fee	na			0.7%
Financial Results				
PV Cost Ratio: Financing / Reins.	1.0	0.6	1.4	2.0
Ratio of: avg. debt service / Premium	1.0	1.9	2.5	3.5

n.a. = Not Applicable
Source: World Bank

The above results show that in present value terms, the cost of utilizing IBRD financing would, over a 200 year period constitute only 60% of the conservatively estimated cost of reinsurance for the specified level of risk. As seen, however, for both IFC and commercial lending (the latter including a small guarantee fee of 0.70%), the long term cost is substantially higher in present value terms (1.4 and 2.0 respectively). The second ratio shown, attempts to demonstrate during any given period of utilizing loan proceeds, what the ratio of debt service (P+I) would be during such period versus having used and paid reinsurance premiums. Such a ratio is useful to determine the level of reserves needed at any time to ensure sufficient liquidity and solvency to repay the required debt service. The following table shows a 400-yr. simulation period for an event probability of 1% (i.e., less frequent but potentially of much larger loss magnitude) using the same financing terms as above, except that the corresponding reinsurance premium at that level would be 4% of the loss coverage layer, given the lower probability of use.

Table 7.7: Testing Alternative Risk Financing Instruments: IBRD, IFC and Commercial Loan Terms Using 1% Catastrophe Event Probability

	Reinsurance	IBRD Terms	IFC Terms	Commercial
Simulation period	400 years	400 years	400 years	400 years
Event probability	1%	1%	1%	1%
Premium Rate	4%			
Interest Rate	na	6.5%	10.5%	11.0%
Commitment fee	na	0.75%	0.5%	1%
Front end fee	na	1%	1%	1%
Maturity/grace	na	15/5	10/2	6/1
Guarantee fee	na			0.7%
Financial Results				
PV Cost Ratio: Financing / Reins.	1.0	0.2	0.3	0.4
Ratio of: avg. debt service / Premium	1.0	3.5	4.8	6.5

Source: World Bank

The second scenario above provides a much more favorable cost/benefit outcome in terms of relative PV costs of using financing versus reinsurance. An additional benefit would be the absence of volatility in the 'reinsurance' rate due to pre-set financing terms. For this purpose, the IBRD loan facility has the additional option of being converted to a fixed rate loan following disbursement through a currency swap/conversion agreement which, under current IBRD policy would only charge a 0.125% fee. At a LIBOR rate of 5.6%, for example, and IBRD's loan spread of 0.55%, the total cost before fixing the rate, would amount to 6.15%. The additional fixed rate cost plus the transaction fee would raise this rate higher, therefore, the 6.5% rate used in the simulation is reasonable and within expected bounds. In addition, the commitment fee assumed is 0.75% while present waivers only require a 0.25% fee payment currently, and in the foreseeable future.

As can be observed, when the lending proceeds are utilized (1% probability), the relative debt service ratio compared to reinsurance premiums is much higher than in the first scenario with 5% probability, and if the loan repayment were annuitized, it would be equivalent to a 13% rate on line. The main reason for this is that, at the 5% probability level and leaving the loan terms unchanged, the premium itself is substantially higher (7% vs. 4%) and therefore the relative debt service ratio in the first case appears more favorable. However, even if this were not the case, there exists another key problem with engaging risk financing at the 5% probability level: At 5% event probability, the excess of loss reinsurance cover represents a low to middle layer cover among the possible layers of cover. At this level, this constitutes a key segment of the XL reinsurance market and therefore using credit facilities, particularly at favorable terms, could constitute market interference. It is therefore not recommended, unless private commercial parties are willing to provide financing at terms similar to IBRD, to engage credit financing for catastrophe risk at the 5% probability layer.

However, the same argument does not apply to the 1% probability layer. This is because at the highest (least likely) but potentially more destructive event probabilities, it is where the global reinsurance market can experience capacity/supply crunches as occurred following hurricane Andrew in 1992. At these upper levels it is precisely where the cat bond market has developed since additional 'capacity' in the capital market exists at these levels. Thus, a more promising use for alternative risk financing and credit enhancement instruments would be at the highest but least probable loss levels which pose inherently risky scenarios for insurers and reinsurers alike. Based on the current insured loss exposure for the OECS, Barbados and Trinidad and Tobago under a pooled structure ($750 mn.), the backstop credit financing requirement would amount to $150 mn. based on the 20% upper level currently reinsured under XL contracts in the region.

However, since the debt service usage under such scenarios implies much higher cash flow requirements (3.5, 4.8, 6.5 as multiples of reinsurance premium for IBRD, IFC and Commercial terms respectively) any such entity, pool or fund utilizing such instruments must have within its financial structure sufficient initial capital to cover the required debt service even if long run costs are lower in PV terms. The latter fact, however, provides the possibility of accumulating reserves at a faster rate so that initial extra capitalization might only need to ensure coverage for the first instance of loan utilization.

Nevertheless, because of the higher debt service costs at the 1% event probability level, in relation to reinsurance premium, the case still needs to be made to determine if use of credit at such levels is indeed more cost effective not only from a cost/benefit viewpoint but also from an annual operating scenario. To do this, the 'savings accumulation' factor was calculated based on the lower cost of utilizing credit in the long run, but also taking into account how quickly those 'savings' accrue before the debt service comes into play. The following illustrates the results of this calculation:

Table 7.8: Accumulation of Additional Reserves Using IBRD Loan Facility to Compensate Higher Debt Service Costs at 1% Probability assuming Mean EPL

	Savings from Loan Facility as Percentage of Previously Paid Premiums under Reinsurance Contract – 100 yr. period	Ratio of accumulated premiums paid versus debt service under using loan facility per 100 yr. Period
Savings accumulation in PV terms immediately before 1% event	81%	5.3
Savings accumulation in PV terms immediately post 1% event, before debt serv.	82%	5.6
Savings accumulation in PV terms, post event and after debt servicing costs	81%	5.2

Source: World Bank

The above shows, as per the earlier analysis of differential present value costs, that the savings from utilizing a stand by credit facility are sufficient to accumulate at a rate which would compensate for the periodic higher debt service payments using a loan facility. Since under the IBRD option, the ratio of debt service to premium was 3.5, the level of savings should be sufficient to build up reserves to pay for eventual loan servicing costs even after including other incidental costs such as administrative expenses. In comparison to the percentage standard deviation of catastrophe reinsurance prices in the last decade, the savings accumulation rate exceeds that significantly, which means that the savings more than compensate for the higher debt service costs (versus reinsurance). Since the savings accumulation provides the necessary funding in disaster years, and since the loan facility maintains a stable cost of financing, this facility effectively reduces the volatility in reinsurance pricing (such reinsurance pricing also rises after major disasters, as discussed previously).

It should be clarified that the above figures assume a constant premium rate for the XL coverage at the 1% risk layer. However, as documented earlier, rate volatility is inevitable and by historical standards, 1998 and 1999, the years upon which the reinsurance rates are based in this exercise, is one of the lowest rate periods in the last decade for the East Caribbean market. The use of credit financing swapped into fixed rates at the highest loss layers, would therefore lock in more stable rates. In this context, multilateral institutional support could only be considered as a catalytic function since permanent support for such a scheme would be expected to be borne by the private markets . It should also be clarified that given the risks that the 1% probability occurs 'early' in the expected cycle, the pool would need to be adequately capitalized initially in the event that the distributions of actual catastrophes become more concentrated than the mean values suggest. The use of debt in this regard has to be measured against the future repayment capacity taking into account the need for adequate initial reserves to accommodate early occurring events.

Figure 7.8: Incremental PV Savings: Credit vs. Reinsurance Cost

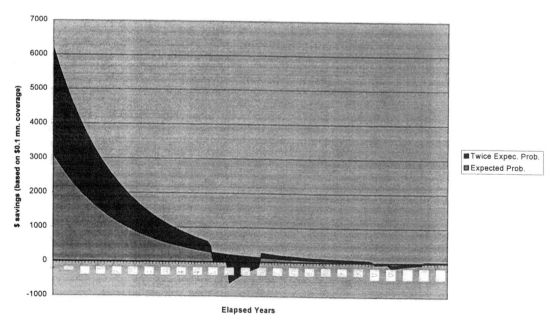

Source: World Bank

To test a more severe scenario, the probability of the catastrophic event was set at double its actuarially estimated frequency so that use of the credit would be twice as frequent over the 400 year simulation period. In this case, even though the 'savings' rate diminishes, the initial accumulation is still sufficient to more than compensate for the cost of debt service following the event. The chart below shows the difference between savings under the mean expected probability scenario and a scenario with a 100% increase in probability.

In the above chart, the "expected probability" (1%) shaded area is of the same magnitude as the 'twice expected' series area except at periods in which the 'twice' series requires additional use of debt service. In such cases, the savings become negative. However, even with this worse case scenario, the initial accumulation of savings (vs. reinsurance costs) is more than sufficient to offset the "dip" years. Therefore, provided that the savings obtained are maintained in a trust or investment account (rather than used for expenditures or paid out as dividends), they would maintain the credit-based cost of reinsurance at a low rate and continue allowing protection against exogenous rate-related volatility.

Eventually, credit support would need to be borne by the commercial market which as shown above, could represent savings of up to 60% in long term premium costs based on a 1% actuarially based event projection. The build up of additional reserves from such savings would also lower the capital 'stress' caused by debt service repayments during 'event' years and this could potentially be ameliorated further by extending the maturity and/or lowering the interest rate further supported by additional credit enhancement mechamisms.

Feasibility of Utilizing Catastrophe Bonds as Reinsurance

The use of catastrophe bonds to support reinsurance capacity for a pool is also considered. At the outset is should be mentioned that catastrophe bonds usually require a number of preparation costs which can amount to 1%-2% or more of the issuance value. These costs pertain to bond underwriting costs and cover the legal expenses, setting up of special purpose vehicles and trusts, ratings analysis, investor marketing costs, and other necessary costs as part of the capital market based transactions. For multi-year bonds, however, these costs can be amortized. If well structured, catastrophe bonds can provide another source of reinsurance capacity with the added benefit of having rates based on the financial markets (e.g.: LIBOR) rather than on global reinsurance capacity alone. In contrast to contingent credit lines, bond coupon interest is payable from the start. In this respect, catastrophe bond payments are more akin to ongoing reinsurance premiums.

As discussed in the earlier chapters, catastrophe bonds to-date, require an above market rate of interest for similarly rated risks. For the upper XL layers under the 1% event probability, cat bonds are being currently priced at LIBOR + 4 (or 9.6%). At the layer below (e.g.: 1%-2% event probabilities) the price is LIBOR + 5.5 (11%). While for investors, the lower probability (upper loss) levels are more attractive given that they imply lower 'default' possibilities, for the 'insured' using such bonds for reinsurance at extremely low probabilities may not be worthwhile since the rate will not necessarily be lower commensurate with the risk (due to the fixed costs of issuing the bond). Bonds which do not protect the principal from loss in the event of a catastrophe that generates losses above the attachment point, are priced substantially higher than those which have principal protection.

In the case of a pooled catastrophe insurance structure for the East Caribbean, it is assumed that credit enhancement support would be required to assure a successful bond issuance for purchase by international investors. As per the earlier analysis, a World Bank guarantee for this purpose would add a 0.7% annual fee to the cost. Therefore, assuming that a catastrophe bond would be used for reinsurance cover at the 0.6%-1% probability level, the total cost to the pool would be LIBOR + 4.7, or at current rates, 10.3%, substantially higher than an equivalent reinsurance premium. However, as per the earlier discussion, the proceeds of a catastrophe bond are to be invested in a trust account in risk free securities. The current U.S. treasury bill rate is approximately 4.9%. Thus, this investment would offset the cat bond financing costs by that amount and provide an approximate net cost of 5.4% = LIBOR + 4.7 – 4.9. So far we have excluded underwriting fees assumed to be an additional one time expense of 2%.

If we use the cat bond form of reinsurance for a $100 million loss limit, the total annual coupon payment 'premium' or rate-on-line equivalent would amount to $5.4 million, and the first year underwriting fee $2 million. In the financing structure of the pool listed earlier, a reinsurance premium of $21 million as a maximum was estimated, even though the current market rate-on-line for the same, would be $3.5 million, i.e., below the cat bond net interest payment. Therefore, based on the projected financial income and expenditure of the pool, a cat bond would still be affordable as an alternative method of reinsurance.

As discussed earlier, though, investors might only be receptive to purchasing such instruments if the loss trigger was clearly defined and transparent. The current loss adjustment process and determination of indemnity payments in any given country might not be perceived as information which is symmetrical in its availability to both the investor and the insured. Because of this, a parametric trigger to determine the claims eligibility is proposed as the only feasible option even though this can generate potential basis risks. Nevertheless, with significant modeling based on hazard intensities at given sites and related dollar losses, a determination of the basis risk could be made. This would require use of meteorological measurements of windspeed and/or earthquake in islands which have suffered from disasters.

For improved 'payment triggering' under a catastrophe bond arrangement, heavy duty wind measuring devices for example, could be purchased and set up in selected spots on each island participating in the pool. These could be connected via wireless transmission to a central database administered by the pool as well as to an independent body such as the Miami Hurricane Center. Once an above threshold wind measurement was recorded, this would serve as the basis for declaring a pre-specified 'loss payment' from the bond, i.e., the bond proceeds would be used to indemnify for affected damages, in which case the investors would lose part of their principal and future interest.

While it would theoretically be possible for the pool administrators in conjunction with the domestic insurers to report exact losses on the ground, and thus allow the cat bond's loss on its principal be pro-rated accordingly, the institutional infrastructure for developing such a reporting system would not only take substantial time to implement, but as mentioned above, might not be attractive as a reporting system to the bond investors. Therefore, loss payments from cat bond proceeds might be structured parametrically as follows:

Table 7.9: Potential Payment Triggers for Multi-Peril Catastrophe Bond

Hazard Intensity Threshold	Investor Loss on Bond for Indemnification
Category 5 Hurricane	80% of Principal
Earthquake Richter 7.5	1.5 % on Interest
Category 4 Hurricane	60% of Principal
Earthquake Richter 6.5	1.0 % of Interest
Category 3 Hurricane	40% of Principal
Earthquake Richter 5.5	0.5% of Interest

Source: World Bank

The hazard event would need to be measured at that level for a specified time (e.g.: 60 seconds or more) at one of the pre-defined sites. The loss of principal and interest, however, would only apply to that portion of the loss pertaining to the country or countries affected. Thus, as in the pool structure shown above, if a category 5 hurricane hit only one country which represented 10% of the total pool exposure, then the loss of the cat bond's principal would be 0.1*(80%), or 8% of face value.

An additional feature that might be built into a catastrophe bond contract is a swap agreement to convert LIBOR based interest payment into fixed rate payments so as to maintain rate stability for the insured and the SPV during the life of the bond. This would also add to the initial funding costs, but as earlier discussed, would still be affordable based on the pool financials. Therefore, in the catastrophe bond instance under such arrangements, a cost versus variance trade off would need to be examined further to determine whether the higher financing costs might indeed offset rate volatility in the reinsurance markets.

Investors have proved to be receptive to catastrophe bonds despite their apparent riskiness. Nevertheless, when compared to similarly (or lower) rated securities in the financial markets, their return versus risk profile is actually much more favorable. Below are shown the relative characteristics of catastrophe bonds with certain attachment probabilities along with other rated securities:

Table 7.10: Comparison of Default Rates on Cat Bonds versus Other Bonds

	Bond Default Probabilities (or equiv. Cat Event Prob.)	Spread above LIBOR
Below Investment Grade Bonds		
Ba2	0.60%	1.10%
Ba3	2.70%	1.36%
B1	3.80%	1.84%
B2	6.79%	2.00%
Principal at Risk Cat Bonds		
Res Re '97	1.00%	5.76%
Parametric	1.02%	4.30%
Trinity	1.53%	4.36%
Res Re '98	0.87%	4.00%
Principal Protected Cat Bonds		
Res Re ' 97	1.00%	2.73%
Parametric	1.02%	2.06%
Trinity	1.53%	1.49%

Source: Goldman Sachs, 1998

In addition to the higher return/risk profile that many catastrophe bonds can offer investors, they also improve the investors overall portfolio risk given that catastrophe bond performance is not linked to global financial market prices since they are based on natural event triggers versus economic/financial factors. Thus, besides the benefits of higher returns, the lack of correlation of cat bond performance with the broader financial markets, improve the efficient investment frontier:

Figure 7.9: Change in Efficient Investment Frontier from Inclusion of Cat Bonds in Portfolio

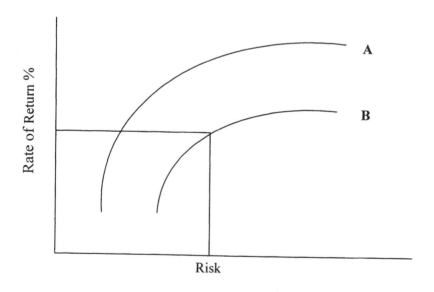

The addition of cat bonds to a portfolio of assets with significant global price correlation, would reduce expected portfolio volatility due to the risk diversification aspect of cat bond returns versus global financial market returns (e.g.: U.S. markets, European markets, emerging markets, in fixed income securities or equities). Thus an equivalent portfolio rate of return can be achieved with a lower risk profile (curve A)

compared to a similarly valued portfolio before adding uncorrelated cat bond securities (curve B).

In conclusion, it should therefore be stated that a number of configurations and options for managing catastrophe risk exist, and these can exploit recent development in risk transfer instruments as well as different capital structures for managing and holding sufficient catastrophe reserves. The structures presented previously for deployment in the ESC case represent what is seen as the most applicable and least complex to implement given the financial participants, country situations, and affordability constraints particularly in terms of fiscal resources available for the payment of insurance premium.

However, in the process of developing a risk management framework for an intra regional group of countries, the risk exposure, insurability, and pricing characteristics may vary once data is collected based on actual conditions and level of resolution used. Such an exercise may well point to alternative structures and funding mechanisms for assets at risk which may need to be seriously considered as additional choices.

This report has attempted to show, however, that under reasonable and conservative assumptions, the case for improved risk management by using a package of policy and financial instruments in the ESC area, can prove to be a valuable policy tool to improve long term development prospects of such nations, as these periodically suffer the devastating effects of natural disasters.

Bibliography

Benfield Greig Ltd.; Working Papers and Analysis of East Caribbean Catastrophe Risk Prepared for the World Bank, September 2000.

CARICOM Working Party, "Working Paper on Insurance and Reinsurance and Catastrophe Protection in the Caribbean", prepared with OAS, World Bank, USAID, May 1996.

Canabarro, E. and Finkemeier, M., Goldman Sachs Fixed Income Research, "Analyzing Insurance Linked Securities", October 1998.

Chase Manhattan Bank, "Financing Natural Catastrophe Risk Exposures", June 1996.

Chase Securities / Chase Manhattan Bank, "Disaster Risk Management for Central America", April 1996.

Cholnoky, T., Zief, J., Werner, E., and Bradistilov, R., Goldman Sachs Insurance, "Securitization of Insurance Risks", April 1998.

Dominica Registrar of Insurance Office, "Commonwealth of Dominica: Report of the Registrar of Insurance on the Administration of the Insurance Act for the Year Ended December 31, 1997".

Eastern Caribbean Central Bank, "1993/1995 Insurance Review".

Eastern Caribbean Central Bank, Draft of "OECS Insurance Act".

Evans, A., "The Insurance and Reinsurance Market in the Caribbean", June 1999.

Fernando, E., Managing Director, Chase Manhattan Bank, "Banking and Governmental Interface in Catastrophic Risk Management", September 1998.

Froot, K., "The Limited Financing of Catastrophic Risk: An Overview", Havard Business School, and NBER, Cambridge, Massachusetts, September 1997.

Froot, K. "The Pricing of U.S. Catastrophe Insurance", Harvard Business School and National Bureau of Economic Research, Cambridge, Massachusetts, March 1997.

Froot, K. "On the Pricing of Intermediated Risks: Theory and Application to Catastrophe Reinsurance", Harvard Business School and NBER, Cambridge, Massachusetts, April 1997.

Froot, K., "The Market for Catastrophic Risk: A Clinical Examination", National Bureau of Economic Research, August 1999.

Gibbs, Tony, CEP Co., "Civil Engineering". Estimates of Vulnerability Reduction Measures.

Goldman Sachs, "Risk Securitization – Opportunities in a Developing Asset Class", September 1998.

Goldman Sachs, "Overview of Investing in Risk-Linked Securities", August 1999.

Guy Carpenter Monitor, "The World Catastrophe Reinsurance Market 1999", October 1999.

Insurance Association of the Caribbean, Statistics Compiled on Caribbean Insurance Premiums by Country, 1998-99.

Insurance Information Institute. N.Y., "Property Insurance in the Caribbean Community", 1997, Prepared for the World Bank.

Insurance Services Office, Inc., U.S., "Managing Catastrophe Risk", May 1996.

Insurance Services Office, Inc., U.S., "Insurer Financial Results: 1998", June 1999.

Insurance Services Office, Inc., U.S., "Financing Catastrophe Risk: Capital Market Solutions", January 1999.

International Monetary Fund, "International Financial Statistics", December 1999.

Litzenberger, R., Beaglehole, D., and Reynolds, C., Goldman Sachs Fixed Income Research: "Assessing Catastrophe Reinsurance-Linked Securities as a New Asset Class", July 1996.

Marsh and McLennan Securities/Guy Carpenter, "The Evolving Market for Catastrophic Event Risk", August 1998.

Millete, M., VP Goldman Sachs, "Introduction to Capital Markets Instruments for Catastrophe Risk Management", September 22, 1998.

Mooney, S., Insurance Information Institute, and World Bank, "Managing Hurricane Catastrophic Disasters in the Caribbean Region through Mitigation and Financial Risk Sharing", June 1997.

Munich Re., Website (www.munichre.com) data on global natural disaster events and costs.

Paterson, D. and Mitchell, A., Beinfield Greig Ltd., Technical Notes on Risk Exposures and Pooling Analysis for the OECS, Barbados and Trinidad and Tobago.

Pollner, J., "Proposed Strategy for a World Bank Role in a Small States Regional Catastrophe Insurance Program", February 1999.

Pollner, J., World Bank Viewpoint, No. 197, "Using Capital Markets to Develop Private Catastrophe Insurance", October 1999.

Pollner, J. and Clarke, L., World Bank and CCMS: CGCED Report, "Wider Caribbean Financial Sector Review", May 1998.

St. Lucia Registrar of Insurance Office, "Report of the Registrar of Insurance for the Year Ended December 31st, 1997".

St. Paul Re., "Average Gross Fire Rates (including Catastrophic Perils) in the Caribbean Region, 1989-1997".

Stubbs, N., "Estimation of Building Damage as a Result of Hurricanes in the Caribbean", OAS/USAID, June 1996.

Stubbs, N., "A Probable Maximum Loss Study of Critical Infrastructure in Three Caribbean Island States", World Bank and OAS, June 1999.

Swiss Re., <u>Sigma</u>, No. 7/1997, "Too Little Reinsurance of Natural Disasters in Many Markets", 1997.

Trinidad and Tobago Supervisor of Insurance Office, "Report of the Supervisor of Insurance for the Year Ended 31st of December, 1996".

World Bank, Working Papers and Analysis of Alternative Financial Structures for Financing Catastrophic Insurance Risks, Pollner, J., Financial Sector Unit, LCSFF, 1997-2000.

Distributors of World Bank Group Publications

Prices and credit terms vary from country to country. Consult your local distributor before placing an order.

ARGENTINA
World Publications SA
Av. Cordoba 1877
1120 Ciudad de Buenos Aires
Tel: (54 11) 4815-8156
Fax: (54 11) 4815-8156
E-mail: wpbooks@infovia.com.ar

AUSTRALIA, FIJI, PAPUA NEW GUINEA, SOLOMON ISLANDS, VANUATU, AND SAMOA
D.A. Information Services
648 Whitehorse Road
Mitcham 3132, Victoria
Tel: (61) 3 9210 7777
Fax: (61) 3 9210 7788
E-mail: service@dadirect.com.au
URL: http://www.dadirect.com.au

AUSTRIA
Gerold and Co.
Weihburggasse 26
A-1011 Wien
Tel: (43 1) 512-47-31-0
Fax: (43 1) 512-47-31-29
URL: http://www.gerold.co/at.online

BANGLADESH
Micro Industries Development Assistance Society (MIDAS)
House 5, Road 16
Dhanmondi R/Area
Dhaka 1209
Tel: (880 2) 326427
Fax: (880 2) 811188

BELGIUM
Jean De Lannoy
Av. du Roi 202
1060 Brussels
Tel: (32 2) 538-5169
Fax: (32 2) 538-0841

BRAZIL
Publicacões Tecnicas Internacionais Ltda.
Rua Peixoto Gomide, 209
01409 Sao Paulo, SP.
Tel: (55 11) 259-6644
Fax: (55 11) 258-6990
E-mail: postmaster@pti.uol.br
URL: http://www.uol.br

CANADA
Renouf Publishing Co. Ltd.
5369 Canotek Road
Ottawa, Ontario K1J 9J3
Tel: (613) 745-2665
Fax: (613) 745-7660
E-mail: order.dept@renoufbooks.com
URL: http://www.renoufbooks.com

CHINA
China Financial & Economic Publishing House
8, Da Fo Si Dong Jie
Beijing
Tel: (86 10) 6401-7365
Fax: (86 10) 6401-7365

China Book Import Centre
P.O. Box 2825
Beijing

Chinese Corporation for Promotion of Humanities
52, You Fang Hu Tong,
Xuan Nei Da Jie
Beijing
Tel: (86 10) 660 72 494
Fax: (86 10) 660 72 494

COLOMBIA
Infoenlace Ltda.
Carrera 6 No. 51-21
Apartado Aereo 34270
Santafé de Bogotá, D.C.
Tel: (57 1) 285-2798
Fax: (57 1) 285-2798

COTE D'IVOIRE
Center d'Edition et de Diffusion Africaines (CEDA)
04 B.P. 541
Abidjan 04
Tel: (225) 24 6510; 24 6511
Fax: (225) 25 0567

CYPRUS
Center for Applied Research
Cyprus College
6, Diogenes Street, Engomi
P.O. Box 2006
Nicosia
Tel: (357 2) 59-0730
Fax: (357 2) 66-2051

CZECH REPUBLIC
USIS, NIS Prodejna
Havelkova 22
130 00 Prague 3
Tel: (420 2) 2423 1486
Fax: (420 2) 2423 1114
URL: http://www.nis.cz/

DENMARK
SamfundsLitteratur
Rosenoerns Allé 11
DK-1970 Frederiksberg C
Tel: (45 35) 351942
Fax: (45 35) 357822
URL: http://www.sl.cbs.dk

ECUADOR
Libri Mundi
Libreria Internacional
P.O. Box 17-01-3029
Juan Leon Mera 851
Quito
Tel: (593 2) 521-606; (593 2) 544-185
Fax: (593 2) 504-209
E-mail: librimu1@librimundi.com.ec
E-mail: librimu2@librimundi.com.ec

CODEU
Ruiz de Castilla 763, Edif. Expocolor
Primer piso, Of. #2
Quito
Tel/Fax: (593 2) 507-383; 253-091
E-mail: codeu@impsat.net.ec

EGYPT, ARAB REPUBLIC OF
Al Ahram Distribution Agency
Al Galaa Street
Cairo
Tel: (20 2) 578-6083
Fax: (20 2) 578-6833

The Middle East Observer
41, Sherif Street
Cairo
Tel: (20 2) 393-9732
Fax: (20 2) 393-9732

FINLAND
Akateeminen Kirjakauppa
P.O. Box 128
FIN-00101 Helsinki
Tel: (358 0) 121 4418
Fax: (358 0) 121-4435
E-mail: akatilaus@stockmann.fi
URL: http://www.akateeminen.com

FRANCE
Editions Eska; DBJ
48, rue Gay Lussac
75005 Paris
Tel: (33-1) 55-42-73-08
Fax: (33-1) 43-29-91-67

GERMANY
UNO-Verlag
Poppelsdorfer Allee 55
53115 Bonn
Tel: (49 228) 949020
Fax: (49 228) 217492
URL: http://www.uno-verlag.de
E-mail: unoverlag@aol.com

GHANA
Epp Books Services
P.O. Box 44
TUC
Accra
Tel: 223 21 778843
Fax: 223 21 779099

GREECE
Papasotiriou S.A.
35, Stournara Str.
106 82 Athens
Tel: (30 1) 364-1826
Fax: (30 1) 364-8254

HAITI
Culture Diffusion
5, Rue Capois
C.P. 257
Port-au-Prince
Tel: (509) 23 9260
Fax: (509) 23 4858

HONG KONG, CHINA; MACAO
Asia 2000 Ltd.
Sales & Circulation Department
302 Seabird House
22-28 Wyndham Street, Central
Hong Kong, China
Tel: (852) 2530-1409
Fax: (852) 2526-1107
E-mail: sales@asia2000.com.hk
URL: http://www.asia2000.com.hk

HUNGARY
Euro Info Service
Margitszgeti Europa Haz
H-1138 Budapest
Tel: (36 1) 350 80 24, 350 80 25
Fax: (36 1) 350 90 32
E-mail: euroinfo@mail.matav.hu

INDIA
Allied Publishers Ltd.
751 Mount Road
Madras - 600 002
Tel: (91 44) 852-3938
Fax: (91 44) 852-0649

INDONESIA
Pt. Indira Limited
Jalan Borobudur 20
P.O. Box 181
Jakarta 10320
Tel: (62 21) 390-4290
Fax: (62 21) 390-4289

IRAN
Ketab Sara Co. Publishers
Khaled Eslamboli Ave., 6th Street
Delafrooz Alley No. 8
P.O. Box 15745-733
Tehran 15117
Tel: (98 21) 8717819; 8716104
Fax: (98 21) 8712479
E-mail: ketab-sara@neda.net.ir

Kowkab Publishers
P.O. Box 19575-511
Tehran
Tel: (98 21) 258-3723
Fax: (98 21) 258-3723

IRELAND
Government Supplies Agency
Oifig an tSoláthair
4-5 Harcourt Road
Dublin 2
Tel: (353 1) 661-3111
Fax: (353 1) 475-2670

ISRAEL
Yozmot Literature Ltd.
P.O. Box 56055
3 Yohanan Hasandlar Street
Tel Aviv 61560
Tel: (972 3) 5285-397
Fax: (972 3) 5285-397

R.O.Y. International
PO Box 13056
Tel Aviv 61130
Tel: (972 3) 649 9469
Fax: (972 3) 648 6039
E-mail: royil@netvision.net.il
URL: http://www.royint.co.il

Palestinian Authority/Middle East
Index Information Services
P.O.B. 19502 Jerusalem
Tel: (972 2) 6271219
Fax: (972 2) 6271634

ITALY, LIBERIA
Licosa Commissionaria Sansoni SPA
Via Duca Di Calabria, 1/1
Casella Postale 552
50125 Firenze
Tel: (39 55) 645-415
Fax: (39 55) 641-257
E-mail: licosa@ftbcc.it
URL: http://www.ftbcc.it/licosa

JAMAICA
Ian Randle Publishers Ltd.
206 Old Hope Road, Kingston 6
Tel: 876-927-2085
Fax: 876-977-0243
E-mail: irpl@colis.com

JAPAN
Eastern Book Service
3-13 Hongo 3-chome, Bunkyo-ku
Tokyo 113
Tel: (81 3) 3818-0861
Fax: (81 3) 3818-0864
E-mail: orders@svt-ebs.co.jp
URL: http://www.bekkoame.or.jp/~svt-ebs

KENYA
Africa Book Service (E.A.) Ltd.
Quaran House, Mfangano Street
P.O. Box 45245
Nairobi
Tel: (254 2) 223 641
Fax: (254 2) 330 272

Legacy Books
Loita House
Mezzanine 1
P.O. Box 68077
Nairobi
Tel: (254) 2-330853, 221426
Fax: (254) 2-330854, 561654
E-mail: Legacy@form-net.com

KOREA, REPUBLIC OF
Dayang Books Trading Co.
International Division
783-20, Pangba Bon-Dong,
Socho-ku
Seoul
Tel: (82 2) 536-9555
Fax: (82 2) 536-0025
E-mail: seamap@chollian.net

Eulyoo Publishing Co., Ltd.
46-1, Susong-Dong
Jongro-Gu
Seoul
Tel: (82 2) 734-3515
Fax: (82 2) 732-9154

LEBANON
Librairie du Liban
P.O. Box 11-9232
Beirut
Tel: (961 9) 217 944
Fax: (961 9) 217 434
E-mail: hsayegh@librairie-du-liban.com.lb
URL: http://www.librairie-du-liban.com.lb

MALAYSIA
University of Malaya Cooperative Bookshop, Limited
P.O. Box 1127
Jalan Pantai Baru
59700 Kuala Lumpur
Tel: (60 3) 756-5000
Fax: (60 3) 755-4424
E-mail: umkoop@tm.net.my

MEXICO
INFOTEC
Av. San Fernando No. 37
Col. Toriello Guerra
14050 Mexico, D.F.
Tel: (52 5) 624-2800
Fax: (52 5) 624-2822
E-mail: infotec@rtn.net.mx
URL: http://rtn.net.mx

Mundi-Prensa Mexico S.A. de C.V.
c/Rio Panuco, 141-Colonia
Cuauhtemoc
06500 Mexico, D.F.
Tel: (52 5) 533-5658
Fax: (52 5) 514-6799

NEPAL
Everest Media International Services (P.) Ltd.
GPO Box 5443
Kathmandu
Tel: (977 1) 416 026
Fax: (977 1) 224 431

NETHERLANDS
De Lindeboom/Internationale Publicaties b.v.-
P.O. Box 202, 7480 AE Haaksbergen
Tel: (31 53) 574-0004
Fax: (31 53) 572-9296
E-mail: lindeboo@worldonline.nl
URL: http://www.worldonline.nl/~lindeboo

NEW ZEALAND
EBSCO NZ Ltd.
Private Mail Bag 99914
New Market
Auckland
Tel: (64 9) 524-8119
Fax: (64 9) 524-8067

Oasis Official
P.O. Box 3627
Wellington
Tel: (64 4) 499 1551
Fax: (64 4) 499 1972
E-mail: oasis@actrix.gen.nz
URL: http://www.oasisbooks.co.nz/

NIGERIA
University Press Limited
Three Crowns Building Jericho
Private Mail Bag 5095
Ibadan
Tel: (234 22) 41-1356
Fax: (234 22) 41-2056

PAKISTAN
Mirza Book Agency
65, Shahrah-e-Quaid-e-Azam
Lahore 54000
Tel: (92 42) 735 3601
Fax: (92 42) 576 3714

Oxford University Press
5 Bangalore Town
Sharae Faisal
PO Box 13033
Karachi-75350
Tel: (92 21) 446307
Fax: (92 21) 4547640
E-mail: ouppak@TheOffice.net

Pak Book Corporation
Aziz Chambers 21, Queen's Road
Lahore
Tel: (92 42) 636 3222; 636 0885
Fax: (92 42) 636 2328
E-mail: pbc@brain.net.pk

PERU
Editorial Desarrollo SA
Apartado 3824, Ica 242 OF. 106
Lima 1
Tel: (51 14) 285380
Fax: (51 14) 286628

PHILIPPINES
International Booksource Center Inc.
1127-A Antipolo St, Barangay,
Venezuela
Makati City
Tel: (63 2) 896 6501; 6505; 6507
Fax: (63 2) 896 1741

POLAND
International Publishing Service
Ul. Piekna 31/37
00-677 Warzawa
Tel: (48 2) 628-6089
Fax: (48 2) 621-7255
E-mail: books%ips@ikp.atm.com.pl
URL: http://www.ipscg.waw.pl/ips/export

PORTUGAL
Livraria Portugal
Apartado 2681, Rua Do Carm
o 70-74
1200 Lisbon
Tel: (1) 347-4982
Fax: (1) 347-0264

ROMANIA
Compani De Librarii Bucuresti S.A.
Str. Lipscani no. 26, sector 3
Bucharest
Tel: (40 1) 313 9645
Fax: (40 1) 312 4000

RUSSIAN FEDERATION
Isdatelstvo <Ves Mir>
9a, Kolpachniy Pereulok
Moscow 101831
Tel: (7 095) 917 87 49
Fax: (7 095) 917 92 59
ozimarin@glasnet.ru

SINGAPORE; TAIWAN, CHINA MYANMAR; BRUNEI
Hemisphere Publication Services
41 Kallang Pudding Road #04-03
Golden Wheel Building
Singapore 349316
Tel: (65) 741-5166
Fax: (65) 742-9356
E-mail: ashgate@asianconnect.com

SLOVENIA
Gospodarski vestnik Publishing Group
Dunajska cesta 5
1000 Ljubljana
Tel: (386 61) 133 83 47; 132 12 30
Fax: (386 61) 133 80 30
E-mail: repansekj@gvestnik.si

SOUTH AFRICA, BOTSWANA
For single titles:
Oxford University Press Southern Africa
Vasco Boulevard, Goodwood
P.O. Box 12119, N1 City 7463
Cape Town
Tel: (27 21) 595 4400
Fax: (27 21) 595 4430
E-mail: oxford@oup.co.za

For subscription orders:
International Subscription Service
P.O. Box 41095
Craighall
Johannesburg 2024
Tel: (27 11) 880-1448
Fax: (27 11) 880-6248
E-mail: iss@is.co.za

SPAIN
Mundi-Prensa Libros, S.A.
Castello 37
28001 Madrid
Tel: (34 91) 4 363700
Fax: (34 91) 5 753998
E-mail: libreria@mundiprensa.es
URL: http://www.mundiprensa.com/

Mundi-Prensa Barcelona
Consell de Cent, 391
08009 Barcelona
Tel: (34 3) 488-3492
Fax: (34 3) 487-7659
E-mail: barcelona@mundiprensa.es

SRI LANKA, THE MALDIVES
Lake House Bookshop
100, Sir Chittampalam Gardiner Mawatha
Colombo 2
Tel: (94 1) 32105
Fax: (94 1) 432104
E-mail: LHL@sri.lanka.net

SWEDEN
Wennergren-Williams AB
P. O. Box 1305
S-171 25 Solna
Tel: (46 8) 705-97-50
Fax: (46 8) 27-00-71
E-mail: mail@wwi.se

SWITZERLAND
Librairie Payot Service Institutionnel
C(tm)tes-de-Montbenon 30
1002 Lausanne
Tel: (41 21) 341-3229
Fax: (41 21) 341-3235

ADECO Van Diermen EditionsTechniques
Ch. de Lacuez 41
CH1807 Blonay
Tel: (41 21) 943 2673
Fax: (41 21) 943 3605

THAILAND
Central Books Distribution
306 Silom Road
Bangkok 10500
Tel: (66 2) 2336930-9
Fax: (66 2) 237-8321

TRINIDAD & TOBAGO AND THE CARRIBBEAN
Systematics Studies Ltd.
St. Augustine Shopping Center
Eastern Main Road, St. Augustine
Trinidad & Tobago, West Indies
Tel: (868) 645-8466
Fax: (868) 645-8467
E-mail: tobe@trinidad.net

UGANDA
Gustro Ltd.
PO Box 9997, Madhvani Building
Plot 16/4 Jinja Rd.
Kampala
Tel: (256 41) 251 457
Fax: (256 41) 251 468
E-mail: gus@swiftuganda.com

UNITED KINGDOM
Microinfo Ltd.
P.O. Box 3, Omega Park, Alton,
Hampshire GU34 2PG
England
Tel: (44 1420) 86848
Fax: (44 1420) 89889
E-mail: wbank@microinfo.co.uk
URL: http://www.microinfo.co.uk

The Stationery Office
51 Nine Elms Lane
London SW8 5DR
Tel: (44 171) 873-8400
Fax: (44 171) 873-8242
URL: http://www.the-stationery-office.co.uk/

VENEZUELA
Tecni-Ciencia Libros, S.A.
Centro Cuidad Comercial Tamanco
Nivel C2, Caracas
Tel: (58 2) 959 5547; 5035; 0016
Fax: (58 2) 959 5636

ZAMBIA
University Bookshop, University of Zambia
Great East Road Campus
P.O. Box 32379
Lusaka
Tel: (260 1) 252 576
Fax: (260 1) 253 952

ZIMBABWE
Academic and Baobab Books (Pvt.) Ltd.
4 Conald Road, Graniteside
P.O. Box 567
Harare
Tel: 263 4 755035
Fax: 263 4 781913